LEAVING CASTRO'S CUBA

The Story of an Immigrant Family

Marina Villa

In memory of my mother, Zeida Villa.
This book is humbly dedicated to the immigrant spirit.

Table of Contents

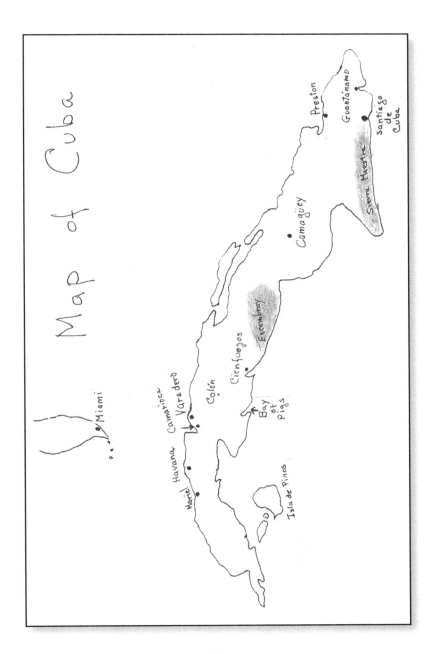

Map of Cuba

Miami
Mariel
Havana
Camarioca
Varadero
Colón
Cienfuegos
Escambray
Bay
of
Pigs
Isla de Pinos
Camagüey
Preston
Guantánamo
Santiago
de
Cuba
Sierra Maestra

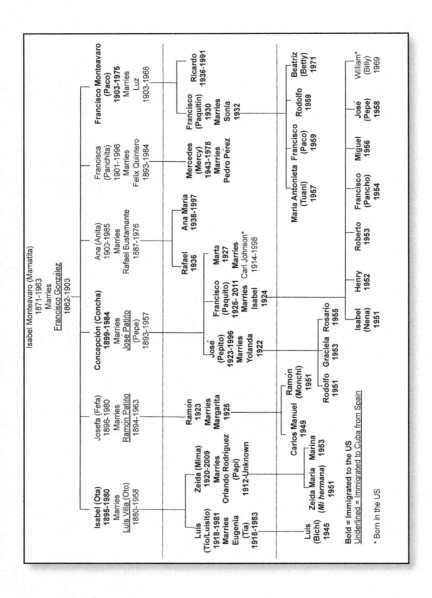

Isabel Monteavaro (Mamatita)
1871-1963
Marries
Francisco González
1862-1903

Isabel (Ota)
1895-1980
Marries
Luis Vila (Oto)
1880-1958

Josefa (Fefa)
1896-1980
Marries
Ramón Patiño
1894-1963

Concepción (Concha)
1899-1984
Marries
José Patiño
(Pepe)
1893-1957

Ana (Anita)
1900-1985
Marries
Rafael Bustamante
1887-1976

Francisca
(Panchita)
1901-1996
Marries
Felix Quintero
1893-1984

Francisco Monteavaro
(Paco)
1903-1975
Marries
Luz
1903-1968

Zelda (Mima)
1920-2009
Marries
Orlando Rodríguez
(Papi)
1912-Unknown

Ramón
1923
Marries
Margarita
1925

José
(Pepito)
1923-1996
Marries
Yolanda
1922

Francisco (Paquito)
1925-2011
Marries
Isabel
1924

Rafael
1936

Marta
1927
Marries
Carl Johnson*
1914-1998

Ana María
1938-1997

Mercedes
(Mercy)
1943-1978
Marries
Pedro Pérez

Francisco
(Paquitín)
1930
Marries
Sonia
1932

Ricardo
1936-1991

Luis
(Tío/Luisito)
1918-1981
Marries
Eugenia
(Tía)
1918-1983

Carlos Manuel
1949

Ramón
(Monchi)
1951

Rodolfo Graciela Rosario
1951   1953   1955

María Antonieta Francisco
(Tuani)   (Paco)
1957   1959

Rodolfo
1959

Beatriz
(Betty)
1971

Luis
(Bichi)
1945

Zelda María
1951

Marina
1953

(Mi hermana)

Isabel
(Nena)
1951

Henry
1952

Roberto
1953

Francisco
(Pancho)
1954

Miguel
1956

José
(Pepe)
1958

William*
(Billy)
1969

Bold = Immigrated to the US
Underlined = Immigrated to Cuba from Spain

* Born in the US

iv

Prologue

Rediscovering Mima

It was Mima's turn.

Judy came to fetch us and mentioned that after the documentary was finished, we would get a copy. She sat opposite Mima at the front of the TV studio, with her back to the camera. Then she instructed Mima. "Zeida, you will be the only one on camera. I will prompt you with some questions that you will then answer in complete sentences. For instance, when I say, 'What is your name?' You will say, 'My name is Zeida Villa.' When I prompt you with, 'Remember when you....', you respond, 'I remember when ...' and explain in detail. Don't answer with 'yes' or 'no,' since my questions are going to be edited out from the documentary. And don't worry if you make mistakes because we can edit that out, too."

"Okay," Mima responded.

The taping began:

Judy: What is your name?

Mima: Zeida Villa

Judy: Where did you emigrate from?

Mima: Cuba

I sat on the side, silently begging Mima to talk in complete sentences. Judy stopped the recording and said to Mima in a gentle tone of voice, "Zeida, you must respond in complete sentences, 'My name is Zeida Villa.' 'I emigrated from Cuba.' Okay?"

Mima acted surprised. "Oooh! I did not know that. Okay, I'll talk in complete sentences."

The recording began again:

Judy: What is your name?

Mima: Zeida Villa

Judy: Where did you emigrate from?

Mima: Cuba

Judy smiled at her.

Judy: When and where were you born?

Mima looked at me. I moved my lips, "1920." I signaled her to look toward the camera.

Mima: Oh, aah…1920.

Judy: Where were you born?

Mima: Oh, in Cuba, of course.

Judy: Zeida, tell us the circumstances surrounding your immigration to the US. Why did you immigrate?

Mima: Well…many different reasons really…

Judy: Zeida, tell me why you left Cuba.

Mima thought for a minute.

Mima: Well, mostly I just wanted my children to grow up in a free country.

Judy: Can you relate the events that led you to want to leave Cuba?

Mima: It was impossible to bring up my children there, so I left.

Judy: Do you remember when you harbored a fugitive in your home?

Mima looked at me with a blank expression. I could tell she was starting to feel uncomfortable.

Mima: Well, there are many things I can no longer remember. My memory is very bad, you know.

Judy: What kind of work did you do in Cuba?

Mima: Oh, I was a math teacher.

Judy: Do you remember when you challenged the Minister of Education?

Mima: No, I can't remember those details. It happened too long ago. I've forgotten...

I lowered my head into my hands. I had held on to the fantasy that Mima was going to be able to tell her story in her own words, but it was not to be. I was frustrated, saddened, and totally discouraged, but Judy was delightful. Never once did she make Mima feel as though she was incompetent. Finally, she said with a big smile on her face, "Okay, Zeida. You did great. Thanks for taking the time to talk with us."

I was so relieved it was over.

Thanks to Judy and everyone else at the local cable TV studio, my mother felt she had done a great job, that she had provided interesting insight into the Cuban situation. As Judy guided Mima down from the stage, one of her colleagues said to me softly, "Alzheimer's is sometimes hardest on the caregivers. I was watching your facial expressions during the interview and I could tell how difficult it was for you. It is very sad to see loved ones deteriorate this way."

I was thankful for his kind comment and his understanding, but what I was most thankful for was that my mother would quickly forget all about this and not ever ask to see the documentary. Thank God!

As we walked back to the car, Mima said, "Well, I think we did something important back there. Someone had to tell the truth about what happened in Cuba. Perhaps something good will come out of it."

I didn't know whether to laugh or cry.

Back home, I looked again through the notes Mima had written so long ago. These formed the basis for a book she had hoped to write. Her Spanish was superb, but it was a US audience that she wanted to reach, and therefore, her notes were mostly in English. On these handwritten pages that had turned brown with age, she came to life for me. The essence of my mother was right there in front of me. I saw how organized her thoughts were. How her principles drove her to make decisions that were courageous and risky. How she took charge of her life and moved on when others might have fallen apart. How she looked after my older sister and me. Yes, I remembered her. She was a remarkable woman. Her uniqueness and strength, her love and her determination, were all there in these pages. Along with her life experiences, she described a world that no longer existed – a world that also murmured in my distant memory.

The contrast between the person who wrote these notes and the person before me was heartbreaking. Entangled in my own issues, I had not given much thought to what my mother had been through in her lifetime. Now, I compared my unemployment

4

crisis to my mother's uncertain future when she arrived in the US to start a new life at the age of forty-five, uncomfortable with the English language, with two daughters and her seventy-year-old mother in tow. No material possessions. No job guarantees. My crisis paled in comparison to what she had faced. She was determined to succeed, and she did.

I did not want her story to vanish. More importantly, I wanted my daughter, who has always been proud of her Cuban heritage, to know the full story. It was up to me to make it happen. The emotional pain from Mima's interview was my wakeup call. I became committed, indeed obsessed, to undertake the project that Mima had once planned for herself, long before she lost her memories. I had her notes, my childhood recollections, and I could find other sources, including many octogenarian friends and family members.

I would write my mother's story – our story - and preserve her legacy.

PART ONE

The Revolution

Zeida with her students in 1948.

Chapter One

Camagüey, Cuba:
September 1965

IT SEEMED AN AFTERTHOUGHT in one of his signature marathon speeches: Fidel Castro said that he would let anyone with relatives in the US leave Cuba. All that was required was for those US relatives to send a boat to the port of Camarioca to pick up their loved ones. I was 12 years old. "Finally, here is our chance," Mima told my sister and me. She explains in her notes:

> *I called my brother in Miami and asked him to send me a boat and to use the $500 he had in deposit for us. A few days later I got a telegram from the government telling me that the boat Seminole would arrive for us, but not to move from my house until I was notified to do so.*

This time it felt real. We had never gotten this close, just waiting for the final authorization. We all knew what to pack. Mima had planned and prepared for years. She had carefully stored in her armoire the clothes we would take, including sweaters she had knitted with yarn from China. She had stood in line for hours at the store for that yarn: red for me, beige for my sister (*mi hermana*). She had also been able to purchase yards of green corduroy fabric, and with it, made two identical outfits. Even though *mi hermana* was almost two years older than I, Mima enjoyed dressing us as if we were twins. We each got a corduroy skirt, a blouse, and a jacket, clothes she made using her own homemade patterns - the days of Simplicity and McCalls were long gone. "We will need to take warm clothes with us to the United States," she'd said. "We don't really know what awaits us there, and even the southern part of the country is colder than Cuba. We need to be prepared."

Mi hermana and I called our friends to tell them the good news. "A boat has arrived for us. We are headed for Miami!" They were happy for us. They came to say goodbye, but they also came to see what we were leaving behind. Can I take your record player? Are you taking this skirt? But Mima had warned us to be cautious. She did not want the neighborhood spies to see anyone leaving our house carrying large objects that, according to the government, belonged to the State. "The record player stays," Mima said. "You can give away some of your clothes as long as they are well hidden. I don't want to have any problems with the authorities." In reality, the old portable record player that Mima had bought second-hand for us years back - the size of two briefcases stuck together – was the only item of value we possessed. Even our records had limited appeal: the 1812 overture, Nat King Cole, excerpts from Carmen.

As we waited for final instructions from the government, however, a complication reared its ugly head. It had to do with our grandmother, Ota. She was notified that before she was allowed to leave, she had to return rent money she'd received from properties that once were hers, but now belonged to the government. Mima writes:

> The total amount was $1,500. I didn't have the money and I wouldn't leave my mother behind. I called a relative who already had a child in the US and I asked him for the amount, that I would pay back to his daughter in the US as soon as it would be possible for me. He gave me $1,500 and I decided not to pay until I receive the notice from the government that the Seminole had arrived. Being afraid of a change in currency, I decided the best thing was to keep the money in the bank. Two or three days afterwards I received another telegram notifying me to be ready in three days. I first took the $1,500 from the bank and paid my mother's debt and then I went to the bank again as the rent for my house, utilities and telephone were supposed to be paid with my savings and the rest would be taken by the government. And then the problem arose. "Why did you take $1,500 from the bank the day before? Didn't you know that from the moment Castro made the announcement until the moment of leaving, no money could be taken from the bank?" It didn't help that I showed them the receipt for the $1,500. I was told that if I was not to return that money to the bank I would not be allowed to leave. I had to be interviewed by a captain

of the army. I was taken to a kind of office in a kind of basement where all the military had long guns and the atmosphere was really scary, at least for me. The captain who was going to interview me happened to have been my student several years back. He recognized me, but that didn't make him nicer. After all the circumstances had been explained, he said, "You cannot leave if you don't put that money back."

Then, I started crying and said, "It is completely unjust that I pay this debt and leave the money in the bank at the same time."

He answered, "Oh, no! The government is absolutely just and right."

I replied, "Then, what I should have done is to keep that money in my house and not to take it to the bank."

"Right," the captain said.

"No," said a representative of the bank who was there, and had also been my student. "The right thing to do was to put it in the bank."

"Well," said the Captain, "we will discuss your case and we will let you know."

I went home completely heartbroken. I did not expect any good reasoning on their part.

Mima looked defeated. I was used to seeing the worry lines in her face, the large rings of sweat under her arms - more from nerves, I think, than from the heat - but I did not expect to hear, when she related the events of the day at the dinner table, that she broke down and cried. I had never seen my mother cry and I could not imagine it. It was her strength that kept us afloat. However, she had already spent three years without a job, relying on income from tutoring at home, an activity considered illegal. And now the stress had built to the point where it could no longer be contained, her formidable endurance had snapped like a rubber band stretched too far, and her emotions, raw and unguarded, were left scattered for all of us to see.

Ota listened intently with her usual frown. She was in charge of putting food on the table. No doubt she was worried about how she could continue to feed us. Thankfully, she did not voice her mantra: "If only there was a man in the family! He would know what to do." I stared at the hills and valleys on the walls - hints of the next chunks of plaster to drop on the floor - and just beyond, the broken spiral staircase we skillfully climbed to hang up laundry and play on the rooftop. I dreaded going back to school the next day. It was a place where *mi hermana* and I did not feel welcome, where the merits of the revolution presided over every academic lesson, and where, lurking over our daily existence, was the imminent reality that at some point we would be sent to the countryside to cut sugar cane. *Mi hermana* seemed a bit less disappointed than I. At fourteen, she was probably somewhat relieved that she did not need to say goodbye to her boyfriend, at least not yet.

The next day, when we returned from school, we found Mima in high spirits again. "We have been given permission to leave!"

The Captain and the authorities had decided in our favor after all.

With renewed energy, we gathered our bags, and then waited, and waited, and waited…

Mima writes:

I went to the bank, all my money was taken (it was not much) and I was left with nothing, waiting for the telegram to come informing us to travel to Camarioca. It never did. Same thing happened to other families. The boats came from Florida claiming specific people and the authorities would embark different people on them. It was such a confusion and chaos that neither the US nor Cuba could stand it anymore. They had to stop Camarioca.

Very soon it was known all over Camagüey that I had no money to survive and friends came to my house offering money. Even a poor woman who had worked for me some time ago, doing the laundry and ironing, came to offer me $20. My mother-in-law came with $100, and some rich families told me, "You only have to ask."

The only money I took was $100 from a good friend who insisted so much that I could not refuse. Luckily enough, some time later I could return it. Some of my money was given back to me.

My students came back, my mother-in-law brought anything she could buy, especially food, and we survived.

It was over. For a brief moment our luck had seemed to turn, and we caught a glimpse of a better life. Now, once more, we were left behind, trapped in a labyrinth of distrust in a place where political loyalty alone established the social order.

Chapter Two

Her Early Years

MIMA WAS A MATH TEACHER and, by all accounts, a member of Cuba's middle class. We lived in the city of Camagüey, but she was born and raised in Cienfuegos in a family of modest means.

Her father, Oto, emigrated from Spain at the age of twelve. He travelled across the Atlantic as a busboy in the galley of a Spanish ship, escaping devastating poverty and an outbreak of cholera in his hometown. Cuba, still a colony of Spain, was known as "The Pearl of the Antilles." The land of opportunities where, it was rumored, gold coins waited to be picked up right from the sidewalks. It was a perfect destination for Spaniards wanting to prosper. Oto settled in Cienfuegos where an older brother lived. Years after his arrival, he became the owner of a small shoe store, and married Ota, who came from a financially strapped but well known family in Cienfuegos. Her father, we were told, was among the first settlers of the city, but he died young, leaving his wife with six young children to bring up on her own. Ota was the oldest.

She was nineteen and Oto was thirty-four years old when they got married. They built a second-floor apartment on top of one of Ota's mother's properties. There, their son Luis was born, and three years later, in 1920, Mima was born. Except for the five years the family spent in Spain, this little apartment was Oto and Ota's home until he died in 1958, on the eve of Castro's victory.

When Mima was three years old, the family moved to Oto's hometown of Santander in Spain. He left the management of the shoe store in Cienfuegos in the hands of two nephews he had sponsored to come to Cuba. He hoped to stay in Spain permanently, living comfortably on the income from his store. But after five years, on the heels of the Great Depression, Oto's store started losing money, and the family was forced to return to Cuba.

"Ay, those years in Spain." I heard Ota say time and time again, "They were the happiest years of my life!"

Soon after their return, Oto had to close his store. On a number of occasions, Ota pawned their wedding rings and other valuables in order to put food on the table. They didn't have enough money to send both children to school, so preference was given to Luis. He was the oldest, he was male, and since his birth, he was the chosen one: he would attend the university and become a medical doctor.

But still, Oto and Ota felt strongly that Mima's education could not be ignored. They were convinced that education enhanced the quality of life, even for women. This was particularly true of Oto, who had to struggle through life without any type of formal education. He wanted both of his children to enjoy opportunities he had not had. So they made the only arrangement they could make: Luis would tutor his sister when he came home from school.

"It was a disaster," Mima told us. "My brother had no patience with me. Every session ended with him yelling and me crying. I could not learn anything!" Ota and Oto quickly concluded that they had to find some other way. Ota asked and prodded until she found a tutor for Mima - a friend of the family who was willing to accept very little pay for her services, often in the form of IOUs or some type of service exchange.

Mima never forgot their first Christmas back in Cuba. Ota, not known for subtlety, said to Mima, "Don't expect to get gifts from the Three Kings tomorrow morning. You are old enough now to know that the Three Kings don't really bring gifts to children. These days nobody can afford to buy toys." Mima did not complain nor make demands, but Oto sensed her disappointment. Late in the evening he called the owner of *El Volcán*, the corner store. "Do me a favor, Román, open the store for a minute so I can get my daughter a little something from the Three Kings." Román was a good friend of the family, and he had a soft spot in his heart for little Zeidita. When Mima woke up the next morning, she found a gift at the foot of her bed – a small mirror, a comb and a hair brush. The magic of the holidays was restored.

Mima often said that Oto, more than anyone else, understood her vulnerabilities. While Ota was the disciplinarian in the family, Oto was quiet, kind, and loving. He was the only one who could resolve conflict and bring harmony when unexpected events occurred that so easily rattled Ota, such as the time the port wine went missing.

Ota had bought an extra bottle of a fine Port wine that she served sparingly to important visitors and to those who provided services that she could not pay in kind. Fearing that Luis would find the bottle and drink it, she decided that the best place to hide it was in Mima's closet. Mima's reputation as a saint was as unshakable as her brother's was for mischief. But one day, Mima noticed the bottle in her closet, opened it, tasted it, and it was good. The wine was so sweet, so delicious, that she kept going back for another taste. She got into the habit of sipping from the bottle each day. She did notice some dizziness in the afternoon, particularly while practicing piano, but after a short nap she was fine and ready for more of that libation.

The day came when Ota went to Mima's closet to retrieve the reserves in order to pour the customary glass of port wine for Mima's piano teacher – a gesture meant to thank him for his patience regarding payment. To Ota's surprise, the bottle in the closet was nearly empty. Ota kept her composure as she served the teacher the last drop of wine, but she was boiling inside.

When Luis arrived home, Ota was waiting for him. "How dare you go into your sister's closet and take the Port wine!" She followed him as he walked by. "Don't you know how much I had to pay for that bottle? Do you think money grows on trees? What am I going to do?"

Luis was puzzled. "What wine?"

"Don't lie to me! I don't know what I have to do to keep things away from you! There is not one safe place in this house, not even your sister's closet!"

Mima was deathly afraid to confess to what now she knew to be a heinous crime. So she did the one thing she could bring herself to do. When Oto sat in the living room after dinner to get away from all the squabbling, Mima sat on his lap, crying, and told him.

"I'm proud of you for telling the truth," he told her. He kissed her cheek. "I'll talk with your mother."

Ota was humbled, Luis was exonerated, and Mima was grounded for a week. She could not go to her grandmother's house in the afternoon to play with her cousins, or take a walk in the evening with her father, or - the highlight of her week - watch the weekly featured movie at *Teatro Prado*, the theatre without a rooftop. But for a girl who always did as she was told, the shame of being punished was harder than the punishment itself. Oto knew this, and each day of her penance he brought her an ice cream after his evening walk.

In time, the family's economic situation improved. Ota had good business sense. She gradually restored solvency to the family through sound investments after the Great Depression and by managing properties for a Spanish family with large real estate holdings in Cienfuegos.

Oto was happy to let his wife take charge. She lived up to the label he bestowed on her soon after they married: "The General," after General Valeriano Weyler y Nicolao, *Marqués de Tenerife*, the ruthless Spanish Captain-General sent to Cuba to crush the independence movement in 1896. He was famously remembered for the way he introduced his mandates: "*Ordeno, mando, hago saber, y que se cumpla!*" - "I order, demand, let it be known, and obeyed!" - a fitting caricature of Ota's style.

As soon as the economic crunch lifted, Oto and Ota enrolled Mima in a regular school. She was an excellent student, and math was her strength. Many of her younger cousins counted on her to help them with their math homework.

Luis, too, was academically gifted. While his conduct caused many disciplinary actions at school, he consistently ranked at the top of his class, seemingly without effort. He was definitely university bound. However, when the time came for him to attend the university, he was not able to do so. This time, the obstacle was not money, but politics.

President Machado, known as one of Cuba's most corrupt rulers – quite the distinction, since every president except the first lavishly used his power for personal gain - closed Havana University to squelch student protests against his government. The university remained closed for almost four years. After Luis spent one idle year waiting for the university to re-open, Ota and Oto sent him to a business school in New York City for a year to learn English. Luis then moved to Preston, a town in the easternmost province of Cuba, to work at one of the two large sugar mills owned by the United Fruit Company.

When the university opened again, Luis had settled in Preston and was romantically involved. He enjoyed a comfortable life and his future at United Fruit was promising. Talk of marriage was in the air. The university was no longer an option he wanted to pursue, despite Ota and Oto's insistence.

Oto then considered sending Mima to the university.

"No! A girl's place is in the home," Ota said. "What is she going to do with a university degree? No! I will not send my daughter to Havana by herself... It is not proper... She will remain right here with me where she belongs." Her most dreaded fear surfaced: "A man does not want to marry a woman with a university degree. If she goes to the university, she'll become a spinster. You'll see!"

While Oto usually gave in to his strong-willed wife, this time he persisted and Ota relented. A new and unexpected course was set for Mima's future.

Chapter Three

A Woman with Two Children

MIMA WRITES:

In 1937, I went to Havana to attend Havana University, where eventually I would get the degrees of Doctor in Education and Doctor in Physical and Mathematical Sciences. The decade of the 30's was noticeable for its economic and political insecurity. After a revolution that overthrew Gerardo Machado's government in 1933 we had all kind of governors, some of them lasting only a few days, and at last, in 1940, Fulgencio Batista, a sergeant in the Cuban army, took the power and became a new dictator. Havana University was like a mirror that reflected this political insecurity. There were riots and strikes and sometimes even killings on the university campus. I developed bad feelings for politics and politicians and decided to stay away from them as much as possible, concentrating on studying.

I was eager to get economic freedom, and enjoy the fruits of my efforts at Havana University, also to release my parents of the expenses of supporting me.

When in 1941 I was hired to teach math at the Instituto de Segunda Enseñanza, the public high school/ junior college in Camagüey, I already had good friends from that city who helped me to break the ice in this conservative society. In a short time I felt at home in the city where I was going to live for the next 25 years.

Camagüey, Cuba, a city of about 100,000 inhabitants and capital of one of the six provinces of Cuba, is one of the oldest cities in the Americas, having been founded in 1511. Its first settlement was on the north coast, but the frequent visits of pirates forced the settlers to move to the center of the island, where (the city) is today. This location, if safer, was also very isolated, especially until the construction of the first railroad trains. Maybe that is why Camagüey kept a traditional ancient Spanish flavor that other cities like Havana and Santiago, founded the same year, have partially lost as a result of their trading with the rest of the world and through the ships that entered and left their harbors.

…The heart of the city, with its narrow and twisted streets, its abundance of churches with towers and bells that could be seen and heard from everywhere, and with its old, big, colonial houses, resembles very much the old Castilian cities.

The houses used to be built around a central patio in which there were a variety of tropical plants, very often birds in cages, and tinajones. These were big pots, some of them bigger than man size, and were used to collect the water that during the rainy season fell from the roof. After the aqueduct was built there was no need for the tinajones, but the people kept them as something typical and traditional, showing them to visitors with utmost pride. The city had the nickname "ciudad de los tinajones." Some families still preferred to drink that water better than that from the aqueduct and people used to say that those who drink it would never leave the city.

Early in the morning, farmers would come into the city selling vegetables, eggs, fruits. Some came in horse carriages, the horseshoes noisily beating against the cobblestones of the street. Others came by foot pushing a cart filled with their products. Housewives would buy the products right at the doors of their homes. At these early hours you could also see women going to church with veils on their heads and missals in their hands.

Bakeries would open early too, as many people would like to have fresh bread for breakfast.

As the majority of the people didn't have cars, there were always people on the sidewalks - some hurrying to their jobs, some waiting for the bus, some chatting in small groups. In the late afternoon or early evenings, very well-dressed women would go shopping or window shopping and men would stand on the sidewalks watching the girls and saying piropos to those who caught their fancy. Piropos are short sentences praising the girls' beauty and grace.

Life passed by, slowly and pleasantly.

In Camagüey Mima met Cuca, and their lifelong friendship started. Cuca taught English at the *Instituto,* and her husband Baldo was the head of the Mathematics Department. He hired Mima from the university. Mima had never met anyone as eccentric as Cuca, and Cuca had never met anyone as kind as my mother. Cuca introduced Mima to another colleague in the English Language Department, Orlando Rodríguez - the man who would be known to me as Papi. At that time he was still married to his first wife.

It was during the following summer, while they both attended classes at Columbia University in New York, that the romance between Mima and Papi started. He was freshly divorced, which put him instantly at odds with Mima's conservative and deeply Catholic upbringing, but he succeeded in gaining her trust, and she fell in love. They announced their plan to marry before returning to Columbia University the following summer.

Ota did not approve at first. "What is she doing, getting involved with a divorced man? The church will not marry them!" But since Papi's previous marriage had been decreed only through a civil ceremony, Ota was appeased by the fact that the Catholic Church would bless this union.

The marriage was not a happy one.

My knowledge of what happened between my mother and father came mostly from Cuca many years later. Papi had helped her when she began teaching at the *Instituto* – a kindness that Cuca never forgot. They had been friends for a long time, but she could not bear to witness how he treated Mima. Although conflicted in her loyalties, after one ugly incident, she finally said to Mima, "Zeida, I don't know how you can stand it. I could not if I were you."

Papi was a very jealous man – a characteristic too common in Latin men of that time, many of whom treated their wives as property, not as partners. Mima was an independent woman, and he was consumed with jealousy every time she engaged in any social activity, with men or with women, if he was not included. He tried to control every aspect of her life, even insisting upon her resignation from the advisory council at the *Instituto* when he, not she, disagreed with the administrative policies.

The situation worsened. Papi often disappeared until late at night, without disclosing his whereabouts. Mima was certain that other women were involved, but she blamed herself; she needed to mold herself into the wife Papi wanted.

Mima kept trying. She hoped that love and patience could turn her marriage around. Once she became pregnant, her focus shifted away from her troubled marriage and towards her unborn child.

She gave birth to a stillborn baby girl. Cuca said she never saw my mother cry, but she could tell Mima was destroyed. During her pregnancy, she had taken the competitive nationwide examinations that would grant her tenure at the *Instituto*. She had attained second place nationwide, but the stress had been intense. Might this have affected the baby? Of course, no one would ever know, but for the rest of her life, she carried this burden.

She soon became pregnant again. She and Papi traveled to Havana so that the baby could be delivered by the finest doctor. But this time the outcome was also tragic. The baby did not get enough oxygen during birth and his brain was damaged. After delivery, she was allowed to see him, but could not hold him. The doctor said, "We can try to save the baby, but he will never be normal. Or we can let him die peacefully."

Mima said, "Please try to do everything you can to save him." He was quickly christened and given the name Juan, and within a week, he died.

Mima and Papi returned to Camagüey and grieved their loss.

She became pregnant for the third time. They again traveled to Havana for the birth of their baby, and this time - on November 2, 1951 – *mi hermana* was born. It was a difficult birth, but Zeida María was a healthy baby.

The happiness around *mi hermana*'s birth did not repair the marital difficulties that had started long before. Prior to her first birthday, Papi again grew increasingly distant. He demanded as much attention from his wife as the new baby, and in its absence, he sought it elsewhere. There were rumors of an affair with a former student. Sometimes he traveled to Havana, not returning for weeks. He rarely came home.

Mima said it was a near miracle that she became pregnant again. This time she spent her pregnancy on her own, with *mi hermana* by her side and someone else who became increasingly close to her: Papi's mother. *Abuela* Mami, in silent disapproval of her son's actions, came to Mima's assistance and support.

When Mima was close to full term, she took *mi hermana*, who was 18 months old, to Cienfuegos to stay with Oto and Ota, so she could travel to Havana to wait for my arrival. Mima told *mi hermana*, "Zeida María, I need you to stay with your grandparents for a short time. They'll take good care of you until I return. They are your other parents."

My poor sister. I can only imagine how horrified she must have felt exchanging sweet, gentle Mima for the General. It was clear that she had taken Mima's words literally: she began to call our grandparents *Otra Mamá* and *Otro Papá*, Other Mom and Other Dad. At her young age, she struggled to pronounce the letter 'r', so *Ota Mamá* and *Oto Papá* stuck. Eventually we shortened their names to just Ota and Oto, and for the rest of their lives, friends, family, and even Mima, her brother, and his family, called them by these names.

In Havana, Mima spent the last weeks of her pregnancy with Ota's sister Concha and her family. June 18, the day when I was born, was *Santa Marina's* day. Mima named me Marina in honor of her aunt Concha, whose real name was Concepción Marina, and also to express gratitude to God for helping her deliver a healthy baby without complications.

She did not dwell on my imperfection: I was born with a rather large, almost jet black birthmark on the back of my head - a birthmark with a surprising story.

A total lunar eclipse occurred while I was in Mima's womb and she, a woman fascinated with science, did not want to miss it. At that time Mima had a maid who was superstitious. She did not have much insight into science and even less knowledge of cosmic events. In fact, Mima explained to her the human reproductive cycle so that she could stop having children. When the maid heard that Mima planned to watch the lunar eclipse, she implored, "*Señora*, please, not in your condition. It is not good for the baby. If you look at the eclipse while your hand is on your belly, the baby will be born with a mark."

"Nonsense," Mima said. "That's *brujería* (witchcraft). There is nothing to worry about and I'll prove it to you."

So Mima watched the breathtaking night sky and convinced the maid, who was also pregnant, to join her. Mima, without hesitation, spread her hand over her own belly and said, "You'll see that nothing will happen."

Her self-assurance was contagious. The maid touched her own belly, but lightly, just in case.

As it turned out, there I was, as the maid had predicted, with a large *lunar*. The maid's baby was born with a much smaller speck. Even Mima had to wonder about this coincidence.

Papi never came back. Six months after I was born, he asked Mima for a divorce. He had fallen in love with another woman. Mima expected it. Cuca told me that she asked him to wait another six months to see what would happen. He refused. He was moving to Havana where his new love lived.

Immediately, Ota asked Mima to return home. Ota was inclined to argue, complain and nag, but when her loved ones suffered, she understood that the role of the family is to support, to bond, to heal. Like rejected merchandise, women typically ended up back with their parents after marital strife.

Mima said no. She was well established in Camagüey. There, also, she had the support of Papi's mother, *Abuela* Mami:

My life was completely dedicated to being a teacher and a mother. Being a Catholic I wasn't allowed to get married again and anyways I didn't want it, first because I didn't want to take the risk of giving a stepfather to my children and second because my marriage had been an awful experience. I lived with my two girls and an old servant in a nice and roomy apartment upstairs from my mother-in-law. This woman, who also was divorced and whose only child was my husband, was an exceptional person. For more than 20 years she had been a teacher at the Normal School of Camagüey and then became the director at a school that belonged to her family, one of the oldest secular schools in the city, founded by her father right after Cuba became independent from Spain. When I got married she built an apartment upstairs from her house for me and my husband to live in.

When my husband, infatuated with another woman, left me, she didn't want me to move out, and told me, "The apartment is for you and your daughters for as long as you want it. It was meant to be for my son and you. He left; you didn't. Now it is your right to stay in it."

From then on, our relationship became closer and closer and in fact, in the 50's, it was that of mother and daughter.

Even with the support Mima received from family and friends, it was not easy for her to adjust to her divorce. That first year, when Mima traveled to Cienfuegos for the traditional Christmas celebration at her grandmother's house, she was apprehensive. She did not know how Mamatita – Ota's mother, in her 80s and the matriarch of the family – would react. Mamatita had always been a source of inspiration for Mima, and now more than ever, because of the similarities between Mamatita's life and her own. Mamatita had been widowed at a young age, soon after her sixth child was born, and she had raised her children without a man by her side.

To her relief, Mamatita told Mima: "Zeida, often we don't have a choice about what our situation in life might be. We could end up divorced, single, widowed, or married, but whatever our fortune or misfortune is, we always have a choice about how we conduct ourselves in that role."

It would be much later - after Castro came to power, after the Bay of Pigs invasion - when Mima fell in love again.

Chapter Four

Castro Takes Cuba:
El Paredón

AT THE AGE OF FIVE I was too young to understand the historic significance of that fateful moment when Fidel Castro claimed victory. However, just like every person in the United States remembers precisely what they were doing when they heard the news of President Kennedy's assassination, Cubans froze into memory the day when Castro toppled Batista, the tyrannical dictator who had assumed power seven years earlier by staging a coup d'état. Mima remembers:

> *Early in the morning of January 1, 1959, I was attending the funeral of the father of a good friend of mine. The atmosphere was the same as other funerals - sad and tired faces, little or no conversation. Suddenly, something unusual began to happen. The faces began to enliven. In a whisper, everyone began to talk. News of something important and of wide interest had descended*

to that place full of sorrow and seclusion. At last, the buzz reached me.

"Batista left last night."

"Is it true or is it another rumor?"

"No, no, this time it is true. It comes from a good source."

The news was so gratifying that it was difficult to maintain the necessary composure. There was, naturally, still some doubt. It was not official - how good really was the source? After the funeral I went to Mass and then home. Upon my arrival, my old maid had the television on and said to me in a state of excitement, "Something has happened, Señora. The TV declared that important news will be announced once it is official."

Finally, around 10:00 am, the news was released: Batista, his family and a few close associates had flown out of the country the night before. This left the way open for Fidel Castro.

Soon the joy in the town was overflowing. From the balcony could be seen how, little by little, everyone went to the streets gesticulating, singing, shouting. Those who were believed to be Batista supporters now seemed to support Fidel more than anyone. Shots were heard and I closed the doors to the balcony. My maid, my two daughters, five and seven years old, and I sat in the room I thought safest in the house and left the radio on to stay abreast of what was happening in the world outside. The first shots were fired in the air in celebration, but one of them killed a well-known medical doctor. This tragic *accident confirmed my decision to remain as protected as possible and for no reason get near the balcony or the windows. Later, more serious explosions could be heard. The army barracks were being attacked by the revolutionary forces.*

At last, the army surrendered and, even though the country at the moment had no government, the celebration continued and the joy in the town was indescribable. Fidel left the Sierra Maestra on his way to Havana to take over the government. He stopped… to deliver a speech to the people of Camagüey. A multitude overflowing with hope went to La Plaza de la Caridad to listen. I turned on the radio but I did not find it interesting and soon turned it off. I was not enthusiastic about Fidel. I was afraid he was just another demagogue, but thought that, nonetheless, he would be better than Batista. The ghost of communism did not enter my mind.

When finally Fidel arrived in Havana, he addressed the people of Cuba through all radio and TV stations. That night I began to listen to him with skepticism, but little by little, I started to become enthusiastic, and at 2:00 in the morning, when he finished, I was one more Fidelista. No, this man is not a demagogue! I thought. He is a patriot! The type of leadership that our island has needed for so long. How fortunate will be this generation to witness the rebirth of our nation!

In the speech that won Mima over, Castro was full of wisdom and in-depth understanding of the political ailments of the past. He wanted to dedicate himself unselfishly to his country. He was eager to bring truth and honesty to the government. He showed a profound faith in the people:

"...No General can do more than the people. No army can do more than the people. I was asked what troops I would prefer to command, and I answered I would prefer to command the people. Because the people are unconquerable and it was the people who won this war, because we had no army, we had no fleet, we had no tanks, we had no planes, we had no heavy guns, we had no military academies or recruiting and training teams. We had neither divisions nor regiments nor companies nor platoons, but we have the confidence of the people, and with this alone we were able to win the battle for liberty..."

He talked about the importance of elections:

"If the team of leaders the present government has does not prove worthy, the people have the right to oust them, not to approve them, I mean in elections, because when everyone knows that they are not worthy, this is the final recourse: elections. We have finished forever here with coups d'état."

He called for establishing long-lasting peace. He was against dictatorship and repression:

"… Now there is no censorship, the press is free and you can be sure that censorship will not be reestablished, ever. Today there is no torture, assassination or dictatorship. Today there is only happiness…"

The entire country was in a euphoric state. *Mi hermana* and I followed Mima's cue, and in our own way, embraced the change that we were too young to appreciate. In some circles, the virtues of Fidel Castro might have been tenuous, but there was no dispute regarding Batista. Everyone thought Batista was evil. The mere intonation of his name was enough to send chills through our bodies. On the other hand, the *Barbudos* - the Bearded Men who fought side by side with Fidel in the *Sierra Maestra* – were virtuous, almost saintly.

The streets were brimming with *Barbudos*. *Mi hermana* and I watched them in awe from our balcony. We got up close to them in the streets, when Mima took us to church, or in the park where we played. She encouraged us to be friendly. Their long unkempt beards were symbolic of the ascetic lifestyle of true revolutionaries, Mima told us. They had endured many hardships fighting a formidable enemy. They had risked their lives and flirted with unspeakable torture just to protect us. They were ready to sacrifice their well-being for ours. It was indeed comforting to see the rosaries around their necks. Our common devotion to God and the church revealed our similarities. No doubt they were on a mission guided by God Himself. *Mi hermana* and I clung to Mima's skirt, smiling shyly, catching a glimpse of the cross dangling from the sparkling beads around their necks. They smiled back, humble and sincere.

We became well acquainted with the faces and the names of our heroes - Fidel Castro, Camilo Cienfuegos and Che Guevara. All were unselfish, brave, untainted by worldly ailments. Fidel, of course, was the leader, and in my mind I placed him next to Jesus, our savior. His two companions were just as heroic. They had led the final offensive across the island against Batista. They were his apostles. It all fit so nicely into my simplistic Catholic framework.

Unfortunately, the honeymoon did not last. It was not long before Mima's doubts began to surface. One of the earlier signs for her, not surprisingly, involved the universities:

> *At that time there were two universities in Havana. There was the old Havana University, which provided higher education to students graduated from the Institutos. Even though it did not provide room and board, the tuition was extremely low (when I was a student it was $45 per year) so that it could be afforded by a great majority of the families. The other one was the private university Santo Tomás de Villanueva. This one was expensive, only wealthy families could afford it and they would accept only the students they wanted. While at Havana University the students were politically active, protected by the university's autonomy, in Santo Tomás the students did not interfere with politics. During the last three years of Batista's regime, Havana University had been closed as the students were on strike protesting against the regime. Santo Tomás stayed open. One of the first rulings of the new government was that those*

graduated from Santo Tomás were required to wait three years for their degrees to be valid. In this way Castro leveled those students with the ones who had lost three years at Havana University.

I didn't like this ruling. I believed then, and still believe, that not everybody serves their country in the same way. Some serve in the most noticeable way of fighting and violence, others in the less noticeable but quite more effective way of learning and improving the conditions of life, working as medical doctors, dentists, engineers, lawyers, teachers, etc. I could not understand what good it was for the country to deny youngsters the chance to work in their chosen profession for three years. But even though I didn't agree, I did not lose my faith in Castro and I thought that he would still do a great deal for Cuba.

Then, war tribunals were formed to prosecute Batista's men who had committed crimes against the people. Many *Batistianos* were imprisoned and most were executed. For hours on end, mobs were heard demanding executions, chanting: "*Paredón! Paredón! Paredón!*" - Execution wall! Mima was disheartened:

I remember watching the trial of Jesús Sosa Blanco on TV. He was accused of the killings of many people in the province of Oriente. The trial was kind of a show. Many peasants (guajiros) were brought from Oriente to Havana and all of them testified how Sosa Blanco had killed and tortured people, but no one had witnessed it.

All of it was hearsay. The atmosphere of the trial was that of a party. People were drinking refreshments, eating peanuts, yelling, laughing, asking for the death penalty. Sosa Blanco said it was a Roman circus. He was right. I felt nauseated and disgusted.

I remember hearing the word "communism" for the first time and I did not know what it meant, but the tone indicated that it was not a good thing. When I asked Mima what it meant, she said, "That's when the government tries to make everyone equal. It sounds like a good idea, but it never seems to work."

I did not quite understand it. Equality was consistent with my mother's behavior. She taught us to treat everyone with respect. She carried on conversations with the janitor at school while most everyone else preferred to ignore his existence. She was visibly affected by the sight of beggars. She had taught our black maid Lucía how to read and write and included her in all family activities. "My white granddaughter," Lucía called me.

I asked Mima, "How can making everyone equal be bad?"

"In reality what happens is that everyone becomes equally poor and the people become unhappy, but they are not allowed to express their views because the government knows what's best," she said.

Chapter Five

Our New Home

IT WAS DURING THESE tumultuous times that Oto died from a mental disorder that we now believe to be Alzheimer's, and Ota moved in with us. Mima's brother's son, cousin Bichi, would soon follow. Schools in his hometown of Preston only went up to the sixth grade, so his parents arranged for him to continue his education at the Maristas School in Camagüey. A notch below the Jesuit brothers in reputation, *Los Hermanos Maristas* was a Catholic order devoted to providing high caliber education in Cuba. Mima's brother had attended the Maristas School in Cienfuegos, and now his son would attend the Maristas School in Camagüey. Where else could he be best cared for than living with his aunt and his grandmother and attending the Maristas?

But the arrival of two new people in our household cramped our living space. The second floor of *Abuela* Mami's house was not large enough for all of us. Mima had built a small house in the suburbs, but it didn't have a bedroom for Bichi. Besides, the house in the suburbs was so far away from *Abuela* Mami and all the schools, that Mima had second thoughts about moving out there without a car. So she decided to rent it out and look for a more conveniently located place in the city.

She heard about an upscale apartment across from the park where she often took *mi hermana* and me to play. But the rent was steep and she was about to rule it out when Ota said, "Zeida, let's go and take a look. If it is right for us, we should take it. I will pay the rent."

"Mamá, the rent is $100 per month. That's too much! We can get something cheaper and still live comfortably."

"Zeida, let's go and then decide."

We all went to see the upstairs of the large bakery across from *Parque Agramonte* and instantly fell in love with it. Even Mima. From the balcony we had a lovely view of the park and the adjacent Cathedral where we attended church every Sunday without fail. When Mima remarked that the light from the three double doors to the balcony highlighted every footprint on the black marbled tiles in the living room, *mi hermana* suggested we only walk on the alternating white tiles. The grownups inspected the details and talked logistics while *mi hermana* and I ran up and down the long corridor alongside the bedrooms.

It wasn't long before Ota said, "Zeida, this is perfect. We are moving in."

The General's orders were clear. We moved into the place. My mother took the bedroom closest to the living room. I shared the adjacent bedroom with *mi hermana*. On the other side of the bathroom was Ota's room, followed by the bedroom carefully prepared for the imminent arrival of Bichi, her beloved grandson – the one now destined to become a medical doctor.

The fifth bedroom remained empty. It was quite unnecessary, Mima maintained. Nobody suspected that within a year, Bichi's parents would need a place to stay.

One of the key selling points of our new home was that it was only two blocks from *Abuela* Mami's house, and we could see her daily.

Handing *Abuela* Mami a key to our new home, Mima said, "My home will always be your home. You can let yourself in whenever you want."

Few people can claim that they were welcomed into a new home with bullets, but that's precisely what happened in our case. I had just arrived from school, and Mima was loosening my school uniform in the long corridor outside the bedroom when we heard the sound of gunfire. A bullet ricocheted off the ceiling, passing inches from my body and lodging itself in the wall. I was clueless about what had just happened. Gunshots and bomb explosions were part of my childhood, and while the sound startled me, I was with Mima and I knew she would always keep me safe. This time, however, there was panic in Mima's face as she gripped my arm and quickly led me into the bedroom. She closed the doors and told me to stay put while she went to find out what was going on.

At the downstairs bakery, an agitated Mima launched into a tirade, "I just moved upstairs with my two daughters and my mother. Someone from this bakery fired a gun in the air and almost killed one of my girls. If you don't believe me, come and take a look at the bullet in my hallway! That has to stop! Innocent people get hurt that way."

The owner came forward, and said, "I'm sorry, Señora. I will deal with the situation. I had no idea you were living there."

"If I hear another gunshot, I will report you. I assure you!" To whom exactly would she report him? It wasn't clear that there was any type of authority, but it was the best threat she could summon.

"It will not happen again. We are very sorry," the owner repeated in a reassuring voice, and he kept his word.

As a peace offering, the bakery delivered an assortment of treats with yet another apology. This is how *mi hermana* and I got hooked on their delicious buns full of raisins and cinnamon, their *capuchinos* smothered in honey – *mi hermana*'s favorite - and my favorite, *napoleones*. How I loved the thin pastry layers filled with creamy custard.

After that, *mi hermana* and I settled quite nicely in our new home. We learned to sleep through the 5:00AM roar of the bakery machinery, and we woke up to the wonderful aroma of fresh baked bread. Thanks to *Abuela* Mami, a loaf awaited us on the dining room table every morning. She was an early riser: "I like to wake up at 5:30, take a cold shower, and go for a morning walk," she often said. "There is nothing more invigorating." After her walk, she stopped at the downstairs bakery, and then dropped off the bread at our house before anyone was awake.

El Parque Agramonte, full of colorful flowers and shade trees, became the daily playground for *mi hermana* and me, but it was not without its danger, as evident by the never-ending application of mercurochrome to my knees and elbows, often followed by gauze and tape for added protection.

Majestic royal palms graced each corner of the park in honor of fallen rebels from Cuba's long history of rebellions and insurgencies. It was a common practice for insurgents to plant a tree in a public area to inconspicuously commemorate their heroes who sacrificed their lives fighting against the establishment. In the center of the park stood a statue of Ignacio Agramonte, a Camagüey native and one of the heroes of the Ten Year's War against Spain. On more than one occasion I attempted to join Agramonte high up on his horse, only to find myself stuck halfway, like a cat in a tree, unable to get down without someone's help.

Mi hermana and I soon found new playmates, Gloria and Rita, two sisters who lived in an apartment building close by. The four of us became inseparable. We delighted in accessorizing our dog, Rondy, using lace and ribbons from Mima's sewing bins. At Gloria and Rita's apartment, we dabbled in make-up and fashion - two commodities that were conspicuously lacking in our home. Gloria and Rita's mother was a fashionable woman, unlike Mima, whose closet was packed with sensible skirts, unmemorable blouses, and practical shoes to match.

Decked out in the latest styles, we took turns walking up and down their patio, noisily clacking high heel shoes too large for our small feet and pretending we were on a fashion walkway. The bright red lipstick invariably travelled from our lips to our clothes and our bodies, making us look more like casualties of war than Vogue beauties, but we felt glamorous.

There were times when we needed someone to aggravate, and there was no better person than Cuca, our mother's dear friend, who lived with her husband Baldo in the same apartment building as Gloria and Rita.

Having firsthand knowledge of Cuca's short temper, the four of us girls delighted in testing her patience. We visited her apartment, and she politely would let us in as though we were adults. She had no idea how to handle children. As soon as she was out of sight, we would raid her refrigerator looking for olives, hide some "priceless" artifact, or play with the black and white balloons hanging from her ceiling, a decór meant to complement her black and white ultra-modern furniture, which was clearly not designed with comfort in mind.

However, our favorite annoying trick was to ring her doorbell and then hide. Cuca invariably appeared at the door wearing North American style flip-flops, skimpy shorts and a provocative halter top, yelling, "You spoiled brats! I know who you are!! Leave me alone!!! *Coño*, I'm going to tell your mother!"

We thought it was hilarious. The more she swore at us, the more fun we had.

Mi hermana and I were always puzzled by the close friendship between Mima and Cuca, since their styles and behavior seemed to put them on different planets. In Camagüey, where respectable women wore knee-length skirts and widows dressed in black for the remainder of their days, Cuca's unique style amused children and scandalized adults. She had been "Americanized." Her frequent visits to the US to attend university courses had made her fall in love with the US lifestyle and the freedoms afforded to women in the States. She adopted US customs at every opportunity, and her choice of clothes –

slacks, halter top, flipflops - attested to this fact. To top it off, her appalling use of language was a contrast to her husband's quiet and traditional ways, and to Mima's sweet nature.

Cuca often commented that no one enjoyed food more than Mima. Of course, Cuca gravitated to the other extreme. Having battled tuberculosis, she looked fragile, almost skeletal. A strong wind could have easily carried her away. For her, nourishment was a necessity, not an enjoyment. In contrast, Mima savored food indiscriminately and tended to be on the plump side, giving her a voluptuous look pleasing to Latin men. No doubt men would have pursued her if only she had been younger, not divorced, without children, without a university degree, and had been at least a little bit *presumida*, a bit more coquettish. But that was not Mima. By nature, she did not seek attention and did not focus on her looks. The one exception to her practical demeanor was lipstick. She would not leave the house without first coloring her perfectly-shaped lips, any more than she would consider not wearing a bra. It was part of her basic attire.

As children, *mi hermana* and I considered Cuca our enemy. She openly criticized how we had taken over Mima's life. "Zeida deserves to have a few minutes to herself. *Coño*, those girls don't leave her alone for one second!" Comments that Mima easily dismissed with her most faithful and timeless companion: a laugh that filled the room with the joyful overtones of an aria gone awry. Then she would say, "Ay Cuca, they are just children. You cannot expect them to behave like adults!" Cuca would grunt in disapproval.

It was true: *mi hermana* and I were quite aware that our mother's world revolved around us. From the moment Mima got home to the time we went to bed, we did not hesitate to impose our demands on her, unless she was convalescing. At times she was confined to her bed, paralyzed by an acute migraine headache. I don't know if her one vice – cigarettes – contributed to her condition, but all too often, her bedroom remained dark. All windows and doors shut. Only Lucía, our maid, was allowed to enter with one remedy or another that never seemed to work. Occasionally, I would sneak in and see her face drained, her energy dissipated, her usual smile dissolved by pain, only the skeleton of her true self before me. I knew it was a transient state. My mother could battle anything, even sickness and pain.

At the age of six, I learned from my mother a most valuable lesson about dealing with conflict.

One day, Rita came to my house with a new toy, a small cradle made out of loosely woven wicker with a rocker at the base, all painted baby blue. It was adorable. Together, Rita and I decorated the frame with colorful ribbons, then we nestled my favorite baby doll in the cushiony bedding we had created, and covered its tiny body with a soft blanket. For a brief moment we both tenderly looked at our creation and basked in its beauty… until the squabbling began for the right to rock the baby doll to sleep. Rita claimed that the cradle belonged to her. I quickly pointed out that the doll and all other accessories were mine. Soon enough, our angelic dispositions coiled into serpents ready to attack. Threats flew. "If you don't let me rock the cradle, I'll take my doll back!"

"I'll take my cradle home and you'll never see it again!"

"I'll never let you play with any of my toys!"

The situation deteriorated quicker than a Middle East peace treaty. Suddenly, I snatched my doll away, feeding bottle and all. Rita said, "I don't need your doll. I have a better doll at my house."

I kept thinking about what else I could do to make her feel miserable and force her to apologize. She was selfish and unfair, and totally undeserving of my kindness and generosity. Here I was, victimized in my own home!

Finally, in desperation, I told Mima. She would make Rita do what I wanted.

She listened to me calmly. Then she said, "Marina, why don't you give Rita the doll? Let her play with it for a while and see what happens."

Her words landed on my ears like screeching nails on a blackboard. Obviously she did not understand the severity of the situation. Capitulate? Never! Why should I do anything nice for Rita? Doesn't Mima understand that I am the victim here?

A few minutes later I thought about it again.

I could not recall my mother ever being wrong. Perhaps I ought to do what she suggested. It was painful. It violated my need for retribution. But I returned the doll and all the accessories. I could scarcely look Rita in the face; with all hope lost, I turned my attention to other things.

To my astonishment, Rita asked me if I would like to play with her cradle again. I felt my anger dissipate. Without an ounce of lingering hostility, we lulled the baby to sleep, picked it up when it was time for a feeding, or a change of diapers, or a shot. We were better friends than ever.

Later, I asked Mima how she knew what to do. "Marina, everything has a better chance to work if you are able to put your anger aside and take the first step to make amends. It can be extremely difficult, I know. Still, you'll see that in the end, it is the best way to get what you are looking for."

In years to come, I witnessed hostilities on a much grander scale between Cuba, the US, and the exiled Cuban community in Miami. Had they had the good fortune to be counseled by my mother, history might have taken a better turn.

Chapter Six

The Revolution's Early Impact

As CASTRO's REVOLUTION transitioned from a rebel's cause to a political movement, laws were enacted in the name of the revolution that defined a new and radical course for the nation. In her customary teaching style, Mima relates one of the first mandates that affected us directly:

> *Then it came, the Reforma Urbana. At the very first moment it only meant that the rents of the houses were cut in half. But let us take a look to the Cuban panorama in this respect. It was the custom in the middle and upper classes to invest in houses as it was a very secure investment if not very productive. The rent of a house might roughly represent 25% of a family income. In a country where there was not social security, a man's thought usually was that if he could buy 2 or 3 houses, in case of his death, his wife could easily administer them*

and manage to survive and raise the children. In this way much of the property was owned by widows whose only income was the product of those rents. To have them cut in half was a serious problem. Once Castro realized this, he changed his first ruling and decided that it would apply only to houses owned by families whose income was more than a certain limit per year.

Now, let us see how this affected me. ... I had moved to a spacious and beautiful home whose rent was $100/ month, a very high rent for Cuba. I had built a small house one year before, which I never lived in, as it was far from where my mother-in-law lived and she did not want us to live far from her. I had rented my house for $50/month. My house stayed making $50/month while the house I lived in, which belonged to one of the richest families in town, was reduced to $50/month. My next door neighbors, whose house was older, smaller and worse than the one I lived in, paid more than I did because they were not lucky enough as to have a wealthy landlord. It had worked very well for me, but I could not help feeling that it was not a just agreement. We were paying rents according to the wealth of the landlords and not according to the quality of the houses we had rented or according to our own income.

The association of Architects complained that these rulings were going to decrease the rate of construction on the island and Castro had a meeting with them. When the meeting was over he addressed the people through a TV channel. It had not been announced, his speech had not been prepared and I happened to listen to it by pure chance. In a state of rage he said things like this: "Why do the landlords think that they are the owners of the houses? They have not put one single brick in them!"

This philosophy astonished me. When he finished I remember I made this comment: "We are in the hands either of a madman or a communist."

It was really the first time I had heard Mima utter words against Fidel and his government. I had sensed disappointment and caution. I had heard doubt and uncertainty, but now the final verdict was in, and it was not favorable.

Everyone wanted to know how the new laws affected your family, your friends, yourself. Cuca framed her sentiments with her usual liberal use of colorful expletives, "*Coño! Carajo!* This is a crime. How can that *hijo de puta* do this?" To my amusement, the rainfall of swears, vulgar phrases, and insults poured out of her mouth with a passion I had never witnessed before – words heard in our home only when Cuca was around.

"Baldo already said that we will continue to pay the Collados the full amount," she said.

Her husband would never express outrage in quite the same way, but Cuca left no doubt about their conjugal solidarity on this issue. "No, this is unforgivable - those *come mierdas* are robbing honest people!"

The Collado family owned and lived in the apartment building where Cuca and Baldo, and also Rita and Gloria, lived. Nobody was more nervous than Paula Collado about the radical political changes taking place. She had moved to Cuba from Spain after the Spanish Civil War, and married into the Collado family, a prosperous family of Spanish descent. The current situation in Cuba brought back memories of the conflicts that sparked the civil war in Spain. She was certain that Castro was communist and feared that Cuba was headed toward a civil war. Paula recounted many tales that horrified us. I remember once she said that people resorted to setting traps for rats in order to have food.

Mima assured me that would never happen in Cuba. "Cuba was blessed with fertile soil, and no political or economic hardship can take that away," she said. "You put a seed in the ground and the next day you can feed your family. Spain is different." Mima knew. She remembered her early childhood there, and while she loved Spain, she did not hesitate to add, "We are very lucky to be in Cuba."

Everyone hoped Paula was exaggerating the threat of communism, but as new laws took effect, fear continued to grow among the middle class.

I was forced to continually categorize and re-categorize the main characters of the Cuban Revolution. Who was good and who was evil, hero or enemy, dictator or savior? Most of the players at one time or another comfortably rested in one of my imaginary compartments, but not Fidel. He defied my classification scheme. Who was he? I wanted to like him. He was brave, intelligent, powerful, and despite my mother's position, I hoped he spoke the truth because I wanted to believe in him. The world around me was divided when it came to judging him. He had done some bad things, but were they errors, or was he really a bad person? What about his heroism? Had he not saved us from the evil tentacles of Batista?

For me, only one other person was as puzzling, so I grouped Castro with him. That person was my father. He had made the mistake of leaving us, but he was a good person because *Abuela* Mami loved him, and she could not love someone who was evil. He was good to *mi hermana* and me on those rare occasions when he came to see us, and while nobody spoke ill of him - particularly not in front of us - I knew from Ota's expression, and by others' reactions to his name, that most people in Mima's circle did not like him. However, Mima had made it very clear that he was not to be criticized in front of her girls. She once walked out of a relative's house saying, "No matter what he's done, he is the father of my daughters and I don't want anyone speaking badly about him in front of my children."

The reality was that, despite the fact that our father was not like other fathers, *mi hermana* and I were drawn to him. Wasn't Castro a similar case? I sincerely hoped that Mima would change her mind about him. What I could not appreciate at the time was that his absolute power controlled our destiny like a puppeteer pulling strings at will, and his ego became impervious to the damage he was inflicting on the Cuban people.

New laws continued to be promulgated. The Agrarian Reform law, the backbone of Castro's revolution, followed the general reduction in rents.

The Agrarian Reform had a broad impact, as it affected the agriculture-based economy of the country. It was an ambitious initiative to redistribute land by capping the size of privately owned farms. Land from large Cuban and foreign-owned ranches and plantations would be appropriated with compensation in bonds.

Camagüey was a large cattle ranch area, and it was heavily affected. Many farmers, in anticipation of having their ranches reduced, slaughtered their cattle in order to sell the meat on the black market. Another law was instituted: anyone caught buying meat on the black market was sentenced to one year in prison.

Within the next couple of years, the rules around the agrarian reform would change. Eventually, small and midsize farmers were also affected and agricultural production became completely centralized under a new government agency, the Institute of Agrarian Reform (INRA). As the redistribution of land spread to the lower end of the economic spectrum, even the small piece of land - probably about 15 acres - that Mima had bought from my father years back was confiscated. Here is the story:

Soon after Castro's victory, *mi hermana* and I heard Mima talk with *Abuela* Mami about this mystery land, and how she had bought it to keep it in the family and pass it on to *mi hermana* and me someday. This made *Abuela* Mami very happy, and made *mi hermana* and me very curious. We pleaded with Mima to take us to see "our farm."

"Girls, it is not a farm. It is just a piece of land. There is nothing to see."

"Let's go anyway...perhaps we can convert it into a farm. We can have horses and cows, chickens and baby chicks..."

"Impossible. I bought it only to make your grandmother happy. Your father wanted to sell it and your grandmother wanted to keep it in the family."

Mima reiterated that we did not really have a farm. No chickens, no horses, no livestock of any kind. In fact, she believed it was covered with Marabú, an insidious undergrowth known as the curse of the Cuban farmer. But *mi hermana* and I insisted, so Mima finally relented, and off we went. The three of us embarked on an interminable bus ride that left us at a grain store. From there, we set out on a long walk. The midday sun was hot; only the shrilling sound of the cicada accompanied us as we trekked single file along the road. I wanted to escape from the heat and quench my thirst, but Mima urged us on. "Come on…remember girls, this was your idea. We are almost there… Just a bit longer."

We came upon a small farmhouse with a thatched roof, and Mima said, "This cannot be the place. We must be lost."

"Mima, let's ask. Perhaps they can give us some water," we begged.

A young woman greeted us and Mima said, "*Ay Señora*, we are lost. Can you point us in the direction of the Larrauri property?" Mima referred to *Abuela* Mami's family name.

"Are you the Larrauris?" The woman asked.

"Yes."

"I think this land belongs to you. Let me call my husband." Mima looked confused.

I pulled at her skirt. "See, Mima, you were wrong. It is a farm!"

The woman invited us in. After giving us cool water from the well, she asked us to wait for her husband. We remained inside, enjoying the coolness from the dirt floor, and holding on to our water like precious gold. Her husband walked in, removed his *campesino* hat and wiped the sweat from his forehead. He shook Mima's hand, and said, "At your service… my wife tells me you are looking for the Larrauri property."

"Yes, we are. Are we in the right place?"

He looked down, "Yes, you are. My wife and I settled here a few years back because it seemed abandoned."

"I'm happy to see that the land is getting used," Mima said. "When I passed by here about five years ago the land was covered with Marabú and I thought it would be impossible to do anything with it."

"It's taken us a long time to prepare the land. It is only now that we've been able to start growing crops."

Mi hermana and I went outside to play while Mima discussed matters with our very own squatters. She assured them that they would not be evicted. They were welcome to stay for as long as they wanted. The husband explained some of the projects he had in mind and Mima said she would pay for materials on the condition that we could come and spend an afternoon at the farm every once in a while.

Each time we visited, there were noticeable improvements to the property. The dirt floor was tiled. They built a barn and added livestock, so we got into the habit of buying chicken feed at the grain store prior to embarking on the long trek to the farmhouse. While Mima inspected and talked with the farmer and his wife, *mi hermana* and I fed the chickens and played in the haystack.

Our last trip to the farm took place after ownership of the property was transferred to the land dwellers. The couple was delighted with the government's actions. Clearly, the two of them felt they deserved to own the land they had worked so hard to farm. Mima understood and she was not really upset, but she was disheartened by their attitude. She sensed bitterness toward her. The redistribution of land had brought to the forefront the class struggle, and the poor people whose needs had been ignored for so long were now the center of attention. Castro had inspired them to become the new voice of Cuba. He had vowed to improve their economic conditions and to eradicate illiteracy, and for the first time in their lives, poor Cubans felt empowered, and played an important part in the success of the revolution. It was natural for them to support Castro and to associate us with the privileged class that Castro incessantly criticized in his speeches. The revolution destroyed the rapport we had built over the years with these farmers, and replaced it with resentment and distrust.

On the international front, Castro was taking steps that would eventually lead to the isolation of the Cuban nation.

Relations between the US and Cuba began to deteriorate as soon as Castro took over the island. To start with, there was the fact that the US had been a strong supporter of Batista's dictatorship, until his government could no longer guarantee the stability necessary for US businesses to prosper. Then there was the issue of the US base in Guantánamo Bay, a sore reminder of the US's continued presence on Cuban soil after its four-year occupation following the Spanish-American war. In addition, Castro repeatedly complained that the US violated international law by not extraditing war criminals - *Batistianos* - back to Cuba. Castro was also infuriated that the US did not stop Cuban exiles in the US from flying over Cuba, sometimes dropping counter-revolutionary propaganda, but occasionally dropping incendiary bombs on sugar cane fields. For its part, the US continued to be troubled by the threat of communism in Cuba, and the confiscation of foreign-owned land without adequate compensation.

There were some conciliatory efforts made on both sides, but throughout 1960, the tension and distrust between the US and Cuba continued to mount. Like spouses in a troubled marriage, each country undermined the other, inflicting lasting damage in the process. Cuba requested weapons from the Soviet Union to defend itself against US imperialism, and Eisenhower launched a covert CIA operation to train Cuban exiles for a Cuban invasion – which would be known later as the Bay of Pigs invasion. The US placed a ban on exports to Cuba. In turn, Castro nationalized all US interests.

Of course, the nationalization of all US interests meant that the United Fruit sugar mill in Preston, where Bichi's father worked, would be taken over by the Cuban government. *Tío* Luis was asked to stay and work for the new government administration. Instead, he chose to resign. Like many other Cubans, *Tío* thought that Castro's regime would be short-lived. He expected the US to intervene within a few months, and his world to return to normal. Until then, he and his wife would move in with us, and endure living under the same roof as Ota. At least they would be with their son.

I remember *Tío* and *Tía's* arrival. A shipment of plants and knick-knacks from Preston preceded them.

Tía arrived full of energy and domestic creativity. She immediately put into practice her decorating talents. Soon, our home, which until now had not boasted a single frivolous ornament, started to assume a more feminine aura.

While *Tía* focused on flower arrangements, porcelain figurines, and avoiding Ota at all costs, *Tío* waited for the political situation to change. He spent his days reading the paper and doing crossword puzzles. The days grew long, and even though he was by nature complacent, his boredom was apparent. He was more than happy to let the women in his life tell him what to do, but when they pulled him in too many directions, he went to a bar for a beer or two.

On occasion, a burst of energy possessed *Tío* and he would take over the kitchen and cook *Arroz con Pollo* with unparalleled gusto. The aroma was the first hint that he was up to one of his cooking frenzies; it filled us with anticipation and teased our noses all day long. When we finally sat down to eat, we were eager to devour every morsel on our plates. His *Arroz con Pollo* was succulent, tender, and flavorful beyond description.

We applauded his culinary talent, although even if the dish had flopped, I think we would have had to celebrate it or risk Ota's wrath. She treated *Tío* as another supreme being, just a notch below Bichi.

Tío reminisced about how he and his buddies in Preston refined and perfected the *Arroz con Pollo* after intensive trials requiring the consumption of many beers. The key secret ingredient, he said – no surprise – was a liberal pouring of that beer.

For the next few days Ota and the maid toiled to put the kitchen back in order, but it was worth it. We were delighted to see a vestige of *Tío*'s true self in action as he fed us memories of a way of life that he would never enjoy again.

Chapter Seven

Becoming *Gusanos*

EVENTUALLY, THE COUNTRY *became deeply divided into two groups, the ones who were devoted and faithful to the regime, and the ones who disagreed with the system and were called gusanos (worms). In the Instituto, where I taught, the students were divided and restless. A group of gusanos planned a demonstration against the regime, and it ended up in a fight between the two factions. Some students were badly hurt. The school administration that before the revolution was elected by the staff among themselves was now appointed by the government. This administration, instead of trying to stop the fight, merely pushed them out of the building to continue fighting. Two teachers resigned as a protest for the way it had been handled. A few days later the school was visited by the Minister of Education. The faculty were called to a meeting where among other things we were told that the teachers who had resigned were working for the CIA and were imperialists whose interest was not the welfare of* the country, but their own. He also said that all teachers were required to declare if they were with the government or against it. This made me feel very bad, as I thought that they did not have the right to ask us about our feelings, and also because the teachers who had resigned were my friends and I knew very well that they were not imperialists, paid by any foreign agency. The meeting was about to adjourn and nobody on the staff had said anything. With a feeling that somebody had to do something, I stood up. Then I heard myself saying, "First, the teachers who have resigned are not imperialists but idealists, and second, I do not agree with the government either so if you want, you can fire me."

The Minister said, "I want to know the reasons for your disagreement with the government."

I replied, "I do not want to discuss them here in this meeting, but if you want, I will discuss them with you in private."

With that, the meeting was adjourned. Next day, when I entered my classroom, I found writings on the blackboard like: "We don't want gusanos," and slogans of the government. Sometimes, at home, the telephone would ring and when I answered all I could hear was a record playing the International or Adelante, the unofficial anthem of the revolution. I learned that the Director of the school had made the comment that he did not know what to do with me, as I was the most qualified teacher in the Mathematics Department and my position *had been earned in National Competitive Examinations, which gave me tenure.*

Mima was shocked that no one else had the courage to speak out at the faculty meeting; nevertheless, she felt compelled to defend the two teachers who had resigned. They were Cuca and Baldo. She thought that once she started, others in the audience would voice their support. Instead, her words were followed by an awkward silence.

"*Ay Caramba!* And where are all those *macho* men when you need them? They act as though they won't put up with anything from anyone, and when the moment comes, not a peep from them. Not one word!"

From that point on, we were labeled *gusanos* – worms - the term coined by Castro to associate his critics with a useless, slimy, low form of life, the scum of the earth.

This did not matter. We were actually proud of our new classification, and I was even more proud of my mother. I always knew she was brave, but now others could see it as well, and she was treated with more respect than ever. Many of her colleagues supported her actions and admired her stance, but only in private.

The day came when she was officially summoned to meet with the Vice-Minister of Education in Havana to discuss her political views. Mima did not know what to expect. She was visibly concerned. She asked our two grandmothers to take care of us if, by chance, she did not return. Before she left, she asked *mi hermana* to make sure to act responsibly, since she was the oldest. Ota notified her brother in Havana to see if he could intervene. He had connections.

Luckily, the meeting in Havana seemed to have been only a fear tactic:

> *They asked why I disagreed with the government. I told them that I didn't believe in fighting ideas with sticks; neither did I like an education in which the students didn't have a choice but to follow the government. I liked the students to be exposed to the different systems and to let them decide by themselves. They did not make any comment, and I went back to Camagüey.*

We were so happy when Mima walked through the door! She had prepared for a long journey, and instead, she was back after a couple days. Mima looked relieved and so were we, now that we no longer had to entertain the notion of a life without her.

At the *Instituto* nothing was the same after that terrible fight between the students. Mima had not witnessed it, but Cuca related the events of that day to me many years later:

Cuca was walking to the school when a group of students ran towards her. They were frightened and bloody, their voices thundering, "Look, *Profesora*, what's happening! The militia is beating us! Go home! It's very dangerous!"

Cuca was horrified. She quickened her pace. Across from the school, the militia, in green fatigues and boots, were clubbing anti-government student demonstrators.

On the steps leading to the entrance of the *Instituto,* two young women screamed, "*Abusadores! Criminales!*"

Cuca took the girls by the hand and said, "It is not safe for you out here. Come inside with me." As she pushed the door, Tomeu, the new government-appointed school Director, held it ajar and told her that she had to enter alone - the students were to remain outside. Cuca said, "*Coño,* Tomeu, you can't do this. It is dangerous out here for the students!"

"Those are the rules. You can come in alone, or you stay out there with the students."

"Ay no… I cannot leave the girls out here… if they cannot come in, I cannot either."

The door closed. Cuca and the girls remained outside. Prepared to protect the girls with her frail frame, Cuca watched the militiamen move closer, their clubs raised and ready to strike. Then a group of students locked arms and formed a blockade to protect them. The militia forced themselves through the line and climbed the steps toward Cuca and the girls. Cuca was not a religious person, but she closed her eyes and prayed.

Meanwhile, Baldo noticed from a second floor window that his wife was at the center of the confrontation. He dashed downstairs and pleaded with the Director to let the women come in, but Tomeu would not budge. A young man ran up to Baldo and handed him a gun. Baldo rushed out of the building with the gun, prepared to defend the women. The militia leader approached him slowly. He looked familiar - Cuca recognized him as a member of a privileged family. He said to Baldo, "Put your gun down and go inside with your wife."

"Not until you back down," Baldo responded. "Don't make me use this gun!"

"We won't hurt the girls. I promise. I will personally walk them home."

Cuca looked at the young militia leader and, with her voice trembling, asked, "Can you swear it? Can you give me your word that no harm will come to them?"

"Yes. We are done here. We just needed to teach the *gusanos* a lesson. I will escort the girls to their home."

Cuca released the girls to him, assured that they were going to be all right, and Baldo put down the gun. But he was upset. He walked up to Tomeu and said, "This is an outrage! I never thought I would see the day when the school would support violent acts against its students. I will not set foot in this school again for as long as I live. As of this moment, my wife and I resign."

Tomeu remained silent. Cuca and Baldo walked away from the *Instituto,* never to return.

A few days later, an emissary from the school was sent to ask them to reconsider their resignation. The entire incident would be forgotten and they would not suffer any repercussions upon their return. Baldo was offered a promotion. Neither Cuca nor Baldo accepted the offer.

The attack on the students was a rude awakening for everyone associated with the school. In the past, the school had provided asylum. It had been possible to voice political differences without fear of brutality. Times had changed: from now on, politics and education went hand-in-hand. The key qualification for becoming the Director of the *Instituto* was the unyielding support of the revolution.

The faculty went along with the system. Some were involved in the underground and wanted to keep a low profile. Some were waiting to leave the country. Most just wanted to live in peace and avoid conflict if they could.

> *That summer, all teachers were summoned for a summer course in Havana, which of course included indoctrination. We stayed in good hotels and the food was better than what we could get at home. About the indoctrination sessions: they were attended by a crowd, and after attending the first one I decided not to go again as nobody would miss me. I met old friends that I had not seen for a long time. They were my friends from the years when we were students at Havana University, but now we were dispersed all around the island. All of them had heard of the problems that we had had in Camagüey. Through some of them I learned that after the faculty meeting with the Minister, he had commented that I might be [from a prominent land-owning family] or in some other way a rich woman who had been hurt by the new laws. After some investigation they found out that I was not. Then the Minister explained my case to Fidel, who said, "That woman wants to be a victim and we cannot allow that."*
>
> *One day my friend and room mate, who used to attend all the indoctrination sessions, told me, "Today they were saying how magnanimous the revolution was,*

that after a teacher had declared her disagreement with the government, she was still allowed to teach."

Of course, I didn't like to be taken as an example of their magnanimity, but that was the last I heard about this incident.

Just short of two years after Castro had taken over the country, he had lost the support of Mima and of the majority of the middle class – a middle class that would not survive Castro's revolution although they had been essential to Castro's victory. It was a middle class that had struggled, endured, and even triumphed, through the many previous political and economic hardships that had plagued the Cuban nation. It was a middle class built by hard-working immigrants, like Oto, who had come to Cuba in search of a better life. Many of them thought that the current situation was not sustainable. They hoped and prayed that they could ride the wave of destruction until its inevitable end.

Chapter Eight

Chaos and Repression

IN JANUARY 1961, the US permanently closed its embassy in Havana and Castro predicted that Cuba was likely to be attacked by a US-led invasion. For the US, the danger of communism in a neighboring nation remained a matter of great concern. For Cuba, the possibility of aggression from the US and the Cuban exile community, together with the emergence of dissident rebel groups within the island country, triggered a defensive and repressive stance.

We were bombarded with slogans. From our balcony we saw youngsters almost as young as *mi hermana* and I, in uniform, marching the streets, chanting:

"*Cuba Sí! Yanqui No!*"

"*Cuba Sí! Yanqui No!*"

Castro's speeches and the Revolutionary Hymn played constantly from loudspeakers in public places.

There were roughly 10,000 political prisoners in Cuba. By the end of March, 1961, close to 100,000 Cubans had left the country, and many of those who settled in Miami were working on initiatives to overthrow the Cuban government. Rebel forces against Castro gathered in La Sierra del Escambray. They waited to act on command from the underground network and undercover CIA agents. Everyone knew a storm was brewing.

Castro swiftly removed from power any individual who criticized the revolution. The free press was abolished. Castro asked maids in every household and workers in public places to come forward and denounce anyone who blurted counter-revolutionary sentiments. The Committees for the Defense of the Revolution (CDR) – also called *comités de barrios*, neighborhood committees - were organized. These were civilians charged to report any type of suspicious behavior in their neighborhood to the authorities. Castro called it a system of collective vigilance. In addition to spying in the neighborhood, the committee was also responsible for gathering "volunteers" to attend public rallies and other government-sponsored activities.

In the *Instituto,* the friction between the students continued to manifest itself, and Mima again became the center of attention:

> *The church was one of the targets of the government and in the Lent of 1961 there was an incident in one church that I didn't witness. The next day in the school some of the members of the student association called a meeting of the students and started telling them how they (the Revolucionarios) had been attacked by the people in the church. Some of the teachers, me among them, listened to the meeting at some distance. Then one of the students went to stand where the others were and said*

that he had been at the church that night and that the people were peacefully praying a via-crucis when they were attacked by government agents. The representative of the student association that had started the meeting insulted the youngster, saying among other things that he wasn't a man (Men were not supposed to go to church and pray to God). This expression hurt me, as after so many years teaching youngsters, I knew how hard it was for an adolescent in our machismo society to be told that he is not a man. So, in a rather impulsive way, [I asked someone beside me, "What is the boy's name?"] Then I went to the stand and I remember that I said, "[Ruben] is a man. He has had the courage to come and say what he saw last night in the church. He hasn't attacked the revolution in any way. Has anyone here heard him attacking the revolution, or only relating what he saw in the church?"

The silence was absolute. The boy embraced me, and the representatives of the association, after saying two or three non-important things, ended the meeting. Next day, I went to my classes as usual. The first class worked out the same as always. For my second class, many students who were not my students asked me if they could attend. I was surprised at this request and especially at the number of students who were asking the same question. I told them, "Of course, you may. As long as you behave you may attend my class."

I still remember vividly, there were about 80 seats in the room and all of them were occupied, plus 40 or

50 students standing against the walls. I couldn't help but ask myself, what is the reason for this? Anyway, everybody behaved and I finished my class. Then, I went to my third class. I entered in the classroom and my usual group of regular students stayed in the hall. The bell rang and nobody entered. I went to the door and I said, "The bell just rang, come in."

I could sense some hesitation in their faces. I asked myself, What is happening? Then two or three students told me, "We have been told by the association not to enter your class. We are scared and we don't want to be the first ones to disobey those orders."

I can still picture how one of the students took his girl friend by the hand and said, "Let's go in."

He did, and everybody came after him. So far as I know, nothing happened to them. For some time afterwards I would find again and again writings on the board when I entered my classes that were not nice to me. Anyway, I felt in some way I was protecting the gusano students by the simple fact of being there and I decided I should not leave the country yet.

While Mima made the decision to stay, many of our family and friends started to contemplate leaving the country. Cuca and Baldo, with no income after resigning their teaching posts, were considering it, at least temporarily until the political situation would changed. Gloria and Rita's family were doing the same, after their father was left without a job because the partners in the law firm where he worked had left the country. Many of the teachers at the *Instituto* were applying for visas.

Bichi's parents started to make plans to leave as well. *Tío* would have preferred to wait a little longer, but for *Tía*, the need for a change was more pressing. She found living under the same roof as Ota barely tolerable. Their relationship had always been strained. But now, our home was consumed by a contest between them for Bichi's affection, and the only beneficiary of this rivalry was Bichi, the golden boy.

Finally, Bichi and his parents went to Havana to wait for the visas that would allow them to leave the country. They expected to return to Preston in a few months, after the US invasion that everyone anticipated.

Chapter Nine

The Bay of Pigs Invasion: April 1961

A FRIEND OF MINE WHO *was in the underground came to see me. He said, "There are three youngsters that we are helping to leave the country because the government is after them and if they get them they will be killed. We had them hidden in a nun's convent but we knew that the convents were going to be searched and we had to take them out. We have found a place for two of them but I have the 3rd in my house, and as they suspect me, I need to find a place for him. Will you take him?"*

I was scared to death but I thought, if they take this youngster and kill him I will never forgive myself. So I took him.

A group of men came to my house pretending to make some repairs and when they left, one of them stayed. I gave him my nephew's bedroom and I said to everybody, even to my mother-in-law, that he was a relative of mine who lived in Havana and came to visit us for a few days. Only my mother knew the truth. My oldest daughter, not yet 10 years old, started asking questions. How was it that she had never seen this relative before or heard of him? I started to get alarmed. The girl was attending school and if she happened to make any comment about a relative she had never seen before, if the comment fell on the wrong ears it could mean trouble. The best thing was to tell her the truth. I called her and said, "We are going to have a woman-to-woman conversation. It is very important that you don't tell anybody anything about what I am going to tell you. When I say anybody it means your sister, your grandmother, your friends. Your mother's life might depend on it." And then I told her the whole story. She never told anything to anybody.

While we were harboring Tito, our fugitive, the US attempt to overthrow Castro began. On April 15, 1961, planes bombed Cuban airfields intending to destroy Castro's feeble air force. Two days later, an invasion fleet arrived at the Bay of Pigs, not far from Cienfuegos. The attack was meant to look as though it was a Cuban plot against Castro's regime, but in reality it was planned and carried out by the CIA, using US aircraft disguised as Cuban Air Force planes, and invaders recruited from the Cuban exile community in the US and trained in Guatemala:

In April 1961, the invasion at the Bay of Pigs took place. Shortly after, the militia was in the streets in big trucks, arresting all those that the Comité de Barrios

[CDR] had denounced as counter-revolutionaries... They didn't have to prove any accusation, and to be counter-revolutionary could mean that in a casual conversation you had criticized some of the government rulings. Pretty soon there were so many people arrested that there was no place to put them. They used schools, churches, any big building available. Many of my friends were arrested that day. Afterwards they told me that living conditions in such places were [inhuman]. The very first day they had nothing to eat. The second day they gave them some Russian canned meat that upset their stomachs. The places where they were imprisoned either didn't have a lavatory or it wasn't enough for so many people. If you think about our hot weather you will understand why the conditions were [inhuman].

My dentist went to a bakery to buy bread for breakfast and didn't come back. Another friend of mine was talking with another friend at the door of his store and a truck stopped and took him. I imagined that the streets should have been completely empty after a while, and I didn't dare to show myself. I told my family, "I am not going to open the door if somebody calls." And I didn't. I didn't go to the front porch. I just hid inside the house.

Baldo woke up to the radio broadcast reporting that US airplanes had bombed certain parts of Cuba. This was the moment he had been waiting for. He immediately got dressed and went out. Within the hour, a young man from the local grain store came to Cuca's door. He said, "I'm delivering the bird seed you ordered."

Cuca knew something was wrong. She did not have birds and she had not ordered anything, but the grain store was the usual meeting place for Baldo and his friends from the underground.

Cuca let the young man enter, and in an agitated voice, he said, "Baldo was picked up by the G2." The G2 was the feared Cuban intelligence police.

"But why would they take him? Baldo has not done anything!"

"The G2 are clearing the streets. A truck stopped in front of the store and took everyone there. I was in the back, so they did not see me."

"I'm going out to find him."

"No, you need to stay here. The streets are not safe."

It was no use. She was determined.

While not directly a member of the counter-revolutionary movement, Baldo had a close association with the local underground organization, a nationwide covert network that was waiting for the US to strike. On cue, they would mobilize against Castro in cities across the island. Cuca and Baldo had hidden large caches of medical and first aid supplies in their apartment for the counter-revolutionary forces, but once they resigned from the *Instituto*, their apartment was no longer considered safe, and the supplies had been moved elsewhere.

Cuca set out to find Baldo. She and Baldo had been detained once before on suspicion that their car had been used to transport arms to counter-revolutionary forces. Cuca's interrogator had said that Baldo was going to be executed. Luckily, the authorities concluded that they had the wrong man. Cuca and Baldo did not own a car. They were let go.

Cuca was convinced that the authorities were looking for a reason to execute Baldo, and she was afraid this was going to be their chance.

She walked to the law offices of a close friend who was also associated with the underground movement. He told her where prisoners were being taken, "But Cuca, please go home. There is nothing you can do about it at this point."

"Nooooo, I'm going to find him before they execute him."

She went to the G2 headquarters and demanded to see her husband, but her request was denied. She feared that without her there, it would be easier to take him out and shoot him. So she said, "I'm going to stay right here until you let him go."

"You either go, or we'll detain you as well." She had no choice but to leave.

Instead of going home, she decided to stay in the shadows across the street from the G2 headquarters. She was ready to jump out of the darkness if she saw Baldo being taken to *El Paredón*. After dark, she sat on the sidewalk and waited. She was not alone. A young man joined her. He was newly married and his wife had been taken prisoner because she was the daughter of one of Batista's men. The young man was nervous, afraid for his wife and for himself. He did not want to go home, so the two of them spent the night sitting on the sidewalk, talking, vigilant of any activity that might be going on in the prison house. Nothing was apparent. In the early morning hours, both Cuca and her companion started to walk home. They hid in the shadows, and as they passed near our house, they witnessed *La Catedral* being ransacked.

When the two were about to go in different directions, Cuca offered the young man her home in case he wanted to hide from the police, but he said, "No, I might as well go to my house and wait for whatever is bound to happen sooner or later."

That was the last she saw of him in Cuba. Many years later she was relieved to find him and his wife walking on the streets of Miami.

Cuca took a shower, packed a few things, and then came to our house because she did not want to stay alone in her apartment.

Mima had to tell her about Tito.

"Zeida, you are crazy. What will you do if the militia comes and finds him here? Who will take care of the girls?" Then Cuca added, "I can't stay. I don't want to bring any more attention to your home."

"Please don't mention this to anyone."

"I won't say a word."

Mima knew her secret was safe.

Within a few days, the US invasion had met its demise. It was an invasion doomed to fail. The air strike had done little damage to the Cuban Air Force because Castro had hidden his few working planes. In addition, the news that the air strike was conducted by US planes using US ammunition reached the U.N. and caused international outrage that discouraged further US support of the attack. The Cuban underground across the country had been eager to join the invasion, but was caught off guard because the CIA never informed them of their plans. Instead, after the first air strike, Castro's militia moved quickly to imprison anyone suspected of counter-revolutionary activities - about 100,000 prisoners, including Baldo. Lastly, the CIA selected a landing site where the invaders could not count on local support. The revolution had greatly improved the standard of living in the economically depressed area near the Bay of Pigs. Castro visited it frequently, and had selected it for one of the first pilot programs to eradicate illiteracy.

Without US air support, and without help from the Cuban counter-revolutionary movement, the invasion was easily defeated and 1,180 of the 1,297 invaders who had landed were captured.

News of Castro's victory quickly dominated the airwaves, and preparations for a big celebration were underway:

May 1st is a great celebration for the communist countries. Several days before, the teachers at the school had a meeting with some government agent. She came to prepare us for the big parade that would take place on May 1st. Among other things she said, "All of you will participate in the parade and I want to remind you that we have full support of the revolutionary army."

I thought that she looked at me when she said this. I thought, of course, I am going. While I have this kid in my house I can't raise suspicions. And so, I went.

The parade was going to pass in front of my house and my mother-in-law's house. Early in the morning a member of the militia came to my house and told me he had to go to the [balcony] with his gun to protect the parade.

My girls were sent to my mother-in-law's house and in my house stayed the militiaman, my mother and my guest who didn't come out of his room.

I didn't feel bad for participating in the parade. I knew that all those who knew me, knew that the only reason I could be there was because I was forced. So, in a way I tried to show myself. It was a hot sunny day. A lady, mother of one of my students, brought me a big hat, one of those used at the beach, and I went to join the parade.

When I passed in front of my mother-in-law's house, she and my girls brought me an ice-cold coke. The parade finished at about 3:00PM: it had started at about 9:00AM and thanks to God there wasn't any reason to complain.

Mima told us to wait for her at *Abuela* Mami's house. We were normally allowed to walk home by ourselves. But nothing seemed normal anymore. Rules kept changing; our lives were riddled with quirks that I could not understand. But after the parade, when she came to pick us up, she radiated a calmness that I had not seen in a long time. I did not know why the parade had been so upsetting but once it was over, she was visibly relieved. The reason – I know now – is that she stopped by our house and found that everything there was okay. The militia man had already left our house and had not discovered Tito. With the invasion and the parade over, Mima loosened up as a robin might after narrowly escaping the eyes of a hawk circling overhead. The worst was over. We were safe. She would no longer shudder every time she heard the doorbell.

Castro's speech on that day, merely two weeks after the invasion, reverberated with confidence. Like the Pied Piper of Hamelin, he led his followers under the spell of his sordid tune. He eliminated elections for the benefit of the people:

"Do the people have time now for elections? No! What were the political parties? Just an expression of class interests. Here there is just one class, the humble; that class is in power, and so it is not interested in the ambition of an exploiting minority to get back in power. Those people would have no chance at all in an election. The revolution has no time to waste on such foolishness."

The one-party system was now in Cuba by decree. Castro had replaced elective government with the "collective leadership by the people" and he, in God-like fashion, became their voice. Using the collective "we," he called for a new Socialist constitution:

"To those who talk to us about the 1940 constitution, we say that the 1940 constitution is already too outdated and old for us. We have advanced too far … That constitution has been left behind by this revolution, which, as we have said, is a socialist revolution. We must talk of a new constitution, yes, a new constitution, but not a bourgeois constitution, not a constitution corresponding to the domination of certain classes by exploiting classes, but a constitution corresponding to a new social system ..."

In this way, Castro established the same political system that he had once denounced - a repressive dictatorship.

> *Several days afterwards I called my friend in the underground and I asked him to take my guest out of my house as everything looked quiet and normal now. Once more a group of men came for a repair job, and when they left there was one more. I had my first gray hairs. Later on, I knew that my guest and his two companions had left Cuba through Caimanera and had arrived safely in the USA. He wrote a letter thanking us and all of those who helped him. I never heard from him again.*

Eventually, most of the Cubans who had been pulled from the streets when the invasion hit were released. Baldo was released after 15 days in prison.

An air of disbelief surrounded us all. Not only were hopes and dreams shattered, but the notion of US invincibility was destroyed. Secretive conversations followed. What to do now? Do we leave the country or stay? If we leave, what are we going to do with our valuables, our pictures, our keepsakes? Mima was careful not to discuss such topics on the balcony or in the living room, thinking people in the street might hear. The back of the house was also not safe, since people from the bakery might hear. Instead, she went to the rooftop with her closest allies to discuss possible options now that Castro was solidly in control of Cuba's destiny:

> ...*many people were leaving the country, the majority of them [going to] Miami. ... Many of my friends had left or were preparing to leave. Many teachers at different schools and at the university resigned and left. For myself, being responsible for two daughters who were very young and my old mother, and being the only person able to work in the group, I decided not to leave yet.*

Those who led the attack were tried on television and interrogated by Castro and other high ranking officials in his government. Mima refused to watch. It was nothing more than theatrics, she said. She was surprised that they were not all executed. Instead, most were sentenced to long prison terms, except for a few who were former members of Batista's brutal police. These were executed.

Chapter Ten

Paquito Goes to Prison

WHILE MIMA WEATHERED the Bay of Pigs invasion with only a few new gray hairs, her cousin Paquito, son of Concha, the aunt who looked after Mima in Havana when I was born, was not as fortunate. He was sentenced to prison for working with the rebel forces against Castro.

Paquito and his brother Pepito lived with their respective families on a large farm in the vicinity of *Playa Girón*, one of the beaches where the Bay of Pigs invaders landed. They did not own the land, but their father had bought the rights to operate it from a large US sugar mogul. Much of Cuba's arable land belonged to a handful of powerful landowners. Some of these were Cubans, but most of them were US enterprises.

When Pepito and Paquito's farm was taken over by Castro's government as part of the agrarian reform, it became an agricultural cooperative under INRA, the centralized agency that was responsible for the overall administration of land redistribution. The government allowed the two families to keep their farmhouses and a small plot of land. Paquito and his wife

Isabel had six children. Pepito and his wife Yolanda had three. The land left to them was, at best, enough to keep them from going hungry and nothing more.

Months prior to the Bay of Pigs invasion, Paquito became involved with the growing resistance against Castro by providing aid to the rebels in the *Sierra del Escambray* – a place identified by the CIA as a possible refuge for the Bay of Pigs invaders, although it was about 100 miles from the landing site, and over difficult terrain. Against his brother's advice, he transported food, clothing, weapons and ammunition to the rebels in his automobile.

A week prior to the invasion, he was at home with Isabel and the children. Isabel recalls the noontime round-up, when a government car came to a screeching halt outside the farmhouse. It was full of armed militiamen, some of them hanging onto the car doors with their machine guns in hand. They surrounded the farmhouse. A militiaman set up a machine gun on a tripod outside the back door, just in case an escape was attempted. "They've come for you," Isabel told Paquito.

"Yes, I know. Let's try to remain calm."

He was prepared. Earlier in the day he had gone to town and heard that an informant had infiltrated one of the rebel groups and had reported the rebels' hideout to the authorities. All the rebels had been captured. He knew it was only a matter of time before they came looking for him.

So now, in front of his children, he was handcuffed and manhandled. His oldest, ten-year-old Isabelita, cried hysterically as her father was taken away. Her mother tried to calm her down, but it was no use.

Isabel then turned to one of the militiamen and asked, "Can I have the keys to the car that are still in my husband's pants pocket?" She was worried because the car provided the only means of transportation to town.

Laughing, he said, "Don't worry about the car. We'll take care of it."

With that, one of the men drove it away. They never saw it again.

On the eve of the Bay of Pigs invasion, a trial was held in the middle of the night at a theatre for all the rebels and their accomplices. Families were not notified. There was no legal representation because lawyers feared the ramifications of defending anyone accused of counter-revolutionary activities, so Paquito acted in his own defense. Most of the rebels, lacking basic literacy, were not as well equipped to defend themselves, but in the end, it really did not matter. They were all found guilty despite the absence of hard evidence. A few days earlier the informant who had turned them in had been shot, while on horseback, by an anonymous rebel sympathizer.

The rebels were all sentenced to thirty years in prison, and their two leaders were executed. Paquito and others who had helped them were sentenced to ten years. Later, all the prison sentences were reviewed and many were reduced. Paquito's sentence was reduced to five years due to lack of evidence and the fact that none of the laborers from the farm had come forth to denounce him.

A few months after his imprisonment, Paquito convinced his wife to flee the country, since she and the children were constantly being harassed by a population encouraged to torment those who disagreed with the government. They joined Concha, and Paquito's sister Marta, both already in Miami. All of them were heartbroken, along with the rest of our family. Every night, Mima asked *mi hermana* and me to say a prayer for poor Paquito.

It was well known that prisoners who were not visited on a regular basis were more likely to be mistreated. Also, prisoners could only maintain marginal health by having a food source from outside the prison. So Pepito convinced his wife Yolanda that they should remain in Cuba to look after his brother, and send their children to Miami temporarily under the care of Concha and Marta. This was possible through a Catholic-run program known as Operation Pedro Pan that allowed Monsignor Bryan O. Walsh, a Miami priest, to issue visa waivers to Cuban children.

Paquito served his prison term. His first six months were spent at the San Severino prison near Colón, a dungeon-style prison in an old Spanish castle. Next, he was transported to *Isla de Pinos*, where he remained for two years, and when that was shut down, he was transferred to Boniato, outside of Santiago de Cuba, where he served the last two and a half years of his sentence.

During the first half of his term, Yolanda scrounged and cooked food to take to him once a month. But after two and a half years away from their children, reuniting with them became her and Pepito's number one priority. They were able to leave Cuba through Mexico, and soon after, joined their children in Miami. Other members of our family took turns visiting Paquito.

Mima visited him once at the Boniato prison. She was shocked by what she saw. He was pale and emaciated. His eyes had a blank stare. It was difficult for him to speak, but as he had done with others who had come before Mima, he forced himself to say, "Zeida, don't come again. I don't want visitors. Next time I will refuse to see you and you will have gone through all the humiliation for naught."

Visiting was indeed a humiliating process. Visitors were stripped naked and their private parts were poked and pried without delicacy or respect, in search of suspicious objects. Their bags of food for the prisoners were inspected and a portion was routinely confiscated by the inspectors. The visitors then walked up a hill with their bag for about a mile in the midday sun, all the while subjected to verbal humiliation from the guards.

Paquito survived the last year of his prison term without visitors, at his request.

Upon his release from Boniato in April 1966, he stopped in Camagüey on his way to Cienfuegos. He arrived late in the evening and rang the doorbell to our home. After a while, without opening the door, a man shouted from inside, "Who is there?"

"Paquito Patiño. I'm looking for Zeida Villa."

"Oh, that *gusana?* She no longer lives here. She left the country a couple of months ago!"

"Very well! Thanks!"

He resumed his trip to Cienfuegos to convalesce at the family's sanctuary – his grandmother Mamatita's house. Soon after, he was able to leave the country and join his wife and children in Miami, where they had their seventh child, Billy.

Chapter Eleven

Aftermath of a Failed Invasion

WHEN IT BECAME KNOWN that three of the Bay of Pigs invaders were Spanish priests, the official crackdown against the Catholic Church began in earnest. Long forgotten was the fact that Bishop Perez Serantes had protected Castro from certain death during Batista's regime, when the army was hunting him down. One of the reasons the middle class and the rich had supported Castro in the fight against Batista was because the church stood by him. But as Castro's government took shape, the church began to openly criticize his regime on the grounds of human rights abuse and loss of freedoms.

The Bay of Pigs invasion gave Castro the ammunition he needed to outright denounce the church that still commanded so much power in Cuba and could provoke resistance against his government.

Castro ordered the expulsion of Spanish priests and proceeded to nationalize all private schools. Most private educational institutions were Catholic, like the Maristas School that every boy from our extended family had at one time or other attended. These schools were mostly run by Spanish Brothers. In Camagüey, *Abuela* Mami's school, which went up to the 8th grade, was one of the only secular private schools, and she had decided to close it soon after Castro came to power. "The revolution is not going to be kind to private enterprises," she said, "and I don't want the government running my school." It was a painful decision because her father had established the school and she had been its director for many years.

On a number of evenings and into the nights, mobs formed in the park, across the street from our home. They banged at the doors of the Cathedral, chanting:

"Paredón pa los curas, paredón!"

"Paredón pa los curas, paredón!"

A mad world was calling for the execution of priests. "The priests are not there!" Mima would cry out inside our home to release some of her tension. In fact, by this time most of them had left the country.

Paredón pa los curas, paredón! Those were the words I heard as I went to sleep, night after night. In the morning, the ugly chant was in my head as I got dressed, and I would repeat it, moving rhythmically through the hallway to the dining room to have my breakfast. Mima, horrified, asked me to stop. "Marina, you are asking for the execution of priests like Padre Basulto. I know you don't mean it, so make yourself stop!"

I had not seen Padre Basulto for some time. Of course I didn't want him to be executed. He was our friend.

Poor Padre Basulto, he had put so much faith in Fidel. Even after the incident at the *Instituto* when Cuca and Baldo resigned, he continued to play the Revolutionary Hymn on the church speakers facing the park. Some might say it was done just to annoy Cuca, who felt it was a personal affront. She could not stand the hymn or Padre Basulto, and constantly complained, *"Coño! Carajo!* Doesn't that *come mierda* ever take a rest from blasting that music out?"

Many of our friends agreed. "Ayyyy Sí! It's unbelievable. It is not fair for him to constantly subject everyone to that horrific sound."

"Coño, one of these days I'm going to destroy those speakers."

But Mima always defended him. "Cuca, he is not hurting anyone...Just ignore it."

"Coño, Zeida, how can anyone ignore that? He is playing that music day and night!"

The animosity between Cuca and Padre Basulto was no secret. Cuca was not a believer, and their political views were at opposite ends of the spectrum, so it was no surprise that the two engaged in some memorable arguments with Mima as referee.

In the end, Padre Basulto's views became closer aligned with Cuca's. After the Bay of Pigs invasion we never saw him again. We heard many years later that he settled in Miami, left the priesthood, and got married.

The failure of the invasion prompted many Cubans, who until then had hope that a US-led invasion would bring an end to Castro's regime, to flee the country. They were leaving their possessions, but more importantly, they were leaving their way of life while still hoping they could someday return:

While I was [in Havana attending a summer course]
my brother with his wife and son left the country, so I had
the chance to go to the airport to say goodbye to them.
It affected me very much. All our lives we had been very
close. I accepted it as the best thing they could do.

Cuca and Baldo prepared to leave.

In October 1961, Baldo received the telegram from the government granting him permission to leave the country. So did Gloria and Rita's family. Cuca's telegram had not yet arrived. There was no reason to be concerned, Cuca thought. She was certain that she would soon get hers, but worried about Baldo's safety, she convinced him to leave without her.

Baldo warned her not to do anything foolish after he left. Cuca assured him, "*Coño*, Baldo, of course I won't do anything stupid! I don't want to create any problems."

Clearly, they had different interpretations of what types of actions were considered foolish. Baldo, the voice of reason, left, and Cuca became fanatically busy giving away all her possessions to family and friends. This was a risky move. The government made it clear that possessions of *gusanos* leaving the country belonged to the state. Later, houses were routinely inspected, but this was not yet the case. It was left to the neighborhood informants, the Committee for the Defense of the Revolution (CDR), to detect suspicious activities. Presumably, if someone was caught giving away their belongings, they would not be allowed to leave the country.

Cuca turned a deaf ear to these warnings. She got rid of all her furniture, piece by piece. Our home was the beneficiary of a couch and a few other ultra-modern accessories. Now our living room featured an assortment of different styles. Mima's soft and cushiony traditional furniture in the far corner of the living room was offset by Ota's austere dark wooden pieces that could have come from Count Dracula's castle. And now in the opposite corner, we entered the space age with Cuca's couch and table.

Then she proceeded to take on her biggest challenge - how to give away her piano without arousing suspicion. She asked her piano tuner if he could help. "Can you tell me how I can get permission to have my piano moved? I want to loan it to a friend until she buys one for her daughter who is taking piano lessons."

He smiled. "I will help you, Cuca. I know what you are doing and if it was me, I might try to do the same. I will arrange the move."

And so the piano was moved. But Cuca did not stop there. She had a key to Rita and Gloria's apartment, so without fear or common sense, she decided to give away some of that furniture as well. Watching from the sidelines, Paula Collado, the former owner of the building and Cuca's dear friend, decided to put a stop to it. "Cuca, you cannot continue this. What if you get caught and you are not allowed to leave? Baldo is already in the US waiting for you!"

"Just a few more things… don't worry, I'm always careful. Nobody will notice."

"Do what you want with your possessions, but giving away other people's things… I think you've gone too far," Paula said. "What if in a few months everything returns to normal and they come back to an empty apartment?"

Cuca thought about it and, although it drove her crazy to leave anything behind for Fidel – that *Puñetero* – she decided that Paula was right. She really should not dispose of other people's belongings. Besides, she had already gotten rid of some key items. She could stop.

A couple of weeks later, when Cuca received her telegram, all her large pieces of furniture were gone. Now she hired an old Chinese man with a wheel-barrel to come to her apartment and move out what was remaining of her possessions, a few at a time. This man would make several trips during the siesta hours to avoid attention. While Cuca had no reason to distrust her helper, she insisted in paying him every day until she left, whether she used him or not, in case he might be inclined to tell the authorities. She spent the last few nights in our home since she no longer had a bed to sleep in. In her apartment, Cuca had achieved extreme minimalism and abstraction: it was empty. She was forever proud that Fidel – that *hijo de puta* - did not get any of her possessions. There had been talk about leaving a bag of cow dung with a sign "Para Fidel," but even Cuca could not bring herself to carry out this obscene, although provocative, idea.

Cuca's fears about Baldo's safety had been well founded. A couple of years later, one of Baldo's closest friends, Marcelino Martínez Tapia, and two other acquaintances were executed in Camagüey after being accused of conspiracy against the government.

PART TWO

Communist Cuba

Zeida with her daughters in Varadero in 1961. Zeida María on the left and Marina on the right.

Chapter Twelve

Living in the Shadows

I HAVE OFTEN STRUGGLED over the merits of the revolutionary message. The ideas are so noble, so utopian, so pure. How can we argue against the literacy campaign, against access to basic healthcare, or for that matter, against a more equitable land distribution that targets the *Latifundios* from colonial times? The problem arises when these worthy causes become agents in the quest for absolute power and control. Everyone gets hurt when the alleged goal is not sincere, even the underprivileged class that the political system so eloquently vows to protect against exploitation.

After the nationalization of properties and businesses, Fidel still insisted that those who accused him of communism were his enemies, even traitors, whose motive was to overthrow the revolution. Many times he adamantly stated that he was not communist. Then, roughly eight months after the Bay of Pigs invasion, he declared his Marxist-Leninist leanings. He said these principles had guided him all along and vowed his commitment to Marxism until the day he died.

The revolution now increasingly encroached into every aspect of our lives. Slogans such as *"¡Patria o muerte!"* and *"¡Venceremos!"* were posted everywhere. Larger-than-life Lenin posters decorated public spaces. With the nationalization of the press, news coverage functioned only as a vehicle for the regime. The newspapers constantly reported the many advances of the revolution, the benefits of the Agrarian Reform, the victory over US imperialism, and the progress of the literacy campaign.

Two manuals were created to launch the literacy campaign: "Venceremos!" and "Alfabetizemos!" Both had an underlying political agenda, spouting the merits of the revolution and condemning the evil empire of the north. The learning materials romanticized *El Líder*, Fidel Castro, hailed Cuba's main benefactor, the Soviet Union, and cursed its nemesis, US imperialism.

Mima's students were expected to "volunteer" to teach reading and writing in rural areas. Graduation was contingent on spending the summer in remote areas teaching basic literacy.

A new concept was at play – volunteering through coercion.

"Volunteers" were actively recruited to cheer Fidel's public speaking marathons in Havana - the revolution's chosen vehicle for governing. Eventually, "volunteers" would be recruited to cut sugar cane. The CDR – the neighborhood watchdog – was the body in charge of making sure there was no shortage of volunteers. After the Bay of Pigs Invasion, the CDR became stronger than ever, monitoring the neighborhood for any type of suspicious behavior and reporting it to the authorities. Who was meeting with whom? What were people saying? Who attended the church services? CDR members had to be informed of all planned social events. They had to make certain that no conspiracies lurked behind seemingly legitimate social functions. So when Mima warned me that a woman from the *Comité* would be coming to my birthday party, I asked the questions that every 8 year old would want to know: "Will I get another present? Will my friends be able to still sing 'Happy Birthday' in English?"

"I doubt she'll bring you a present, Marina, but I don't see a problem with 'Happy Birthday.' Make sure to bring her a piece of cake afterwards." So I did.

For their exemplary service to the revolution, CDR members were rewarded in many ways: better jobs, relatively good access to food and other staples, such as toilet paper. Their absence from the long lines at the stores was noticeable. The Socio-economic stratification would no longer be defined by wealth. Instead, it would be linked to unwavering allegiance to government demands.

Sunday Mass was the only time we escaped this new world of Socialism, Leninism, and Marxism. At the church we still had the calming presence of the Virgin Mary. While the *pioneros*, the children of the revolution, shouted militant chants in perfect unison -- *Cuba sí! Yanqui no!* -- I marveled at the peaceful beauty of baroque frescoes that graced the high ceilings of *La Iglesia de la Soledad*, and tuned to the soothing voices from the choir bouncing off the empty pews.

All television programming contained a revolutionary message. The Adventures of Robin Hood became my favorite TV show. What better propaganda could there be for the revolution than to compare it to a romantic hero who stole from the rich to help the poor?

Hollywood movies vanished. Oh, how I missed the Disney movies, and romantic comedies such as "Some Like it Hot." The Soviet bloc films were dark – literally, since all were black and white - and sobering, with no notion of happy-ever-after. No music, no humor, just one overwhelming class struggle, where children were taken from their parents, laborers were treated as slaves, women were abused, and after a successful but bloody revolt, the survivors, amidst all the devastation, pledged allegiance to the new order. Who would want to escape reality in this way?

The Revolutionary Hymn and the International Anthem replaced *La Música Criolla de Cuba*. Yes, the repression extended to the acclaimed Afro-Cuban music widely enjoyed today. As in China's Cultural Revolution, music without a revolutionary message, or in some way symbolic of pre-revolutionary times, was by default counter-revolutionary, and not allowed. The rich sounds of Afro-Cuban music were repressed for many years. Its revival came much later, when it was discovered as a way to promote Cuba abroad, and thereby benefiting the revolution.

Throughout Camagüey there was an emergence of foreigners after the botched Bay of Pigs invasion. Some of them were visiting priests from Europe – many from Belgium - who took the place of the banished Spanish priests. You might imagine my surprise the first time I attended a church service with Mima where I failed to understand a word of the sermon.

"Was it in Latin?" I asked Mima on our way home.

Mima laughed. "Ay Marina, no, that was Spanish. The new priests are still learning the language." In her most reassuring voice, she added, "Soon you'll understand every word. You'll see. They will improve, and you'll get used to hearing their pronunciation."

I don't think anyone ever fully understood the new priests, but those Cubans who still attended church services, never short of imagination, sat quietly in the pews listening, grateful that these priests had come to help during their hour of need. They had been allowed to come to Cuba because, unlike the Spanish priests, they were not integrated into the social fabric of the country, and therefore were not in a position to encourage political dissent among parishioners. Their only goal was to provide spiritual solace to the diminishing number of Cuban Catholics – those who had not left the country, and who were not afraid to attend services.

Most other foreigners were Soviets – most likely "volunteers" - who had come to Cuba to aid the revolutionary cause. Many were technicians, attempting to help with the agricultural initiatives in general and with the sugar industry in particular. The sugar production had depended on US equipment operated by Cubans who, for the most part, had left the country. The Soviet technicians were expected to help fill the technical gap. They did not speak Spanish and Cubans could not speak Russian so, ironically, a rudimentary English dialect became the common language between the two cultures.

The Soviets lived in their own camps, away from Cubans. Occasionally *mi hermana* and I saw them in town, tall and fair, and expressionless. We tried to listen to their conversation, but while Cubans talk constantly, these guys were reserved, almost lacking human – or, perhaps more accurately, Cuban - emotions. Not surprisingly, their serious and detached demeanor was interpreted as unfriendliness.

We heard rumors that they concocted their own alcoholic beverage using pharmaceutical ingredients. Cubans were certain that a sip of this brew would kill any Cuban on the spot. Their reputation had preceded them with the various products now imported from Russia, particularly the abysmal canned meat that often caused gastrointestinal pains. Indeed, it was difficult to trust the Soviets with fixing the agricultural problems in Cuba, based on the goods imported from their country. In our home, Rondy, the dog, became the main consumer of Russian canned meat, and Ota found another weapon to use on *mi hermana* and me: "You better behave, or I'll serve Russian meat for dinner!"

But soon enough, we would wish we had Russian canned meat to eat.

The loss of the US market, and payment to the Soviets for weapons, were taking a toll on the economic viability of the nation. The US ban on exports to Cuba prevented Cuba from obtaining replacement parts for the US machinery in sugar mills and other agricultural centers. In addition, agricultural production and the drive towards agricultural diversification under the Agrarian Reform Institute (INRA) were severely mismanaged, leading to waste and misuse that jumpstarted a downward spiral that continues to plague the country even now, fifty years later.

In the near future, there would be virtually no goods for sale. Mima would be forced to give up one of her most gratifying habits - the demitasse of Cuban coffee after her afternoon *siesta*. Instead, she settled for burnt sugar mixed with water. And in Camagüey, the heart of Cuba's cattle region, it would be impossible to buy beef.

Chapter Thirteen

Love Story

IT WAS AROUND THIS time, after so many of our friends and relatives had left the country, that I found Mima often distracted in her thoughts. It was bound to happen: Mima had fallen in love again. Walking home from church on numerous occasions, we ran into him, and he walked with us, the two of them oblivious to the world around them, tuned into each other as they carried on what seemed to me idle - and intensely boring - conversations. He was a teacher at the *Instituto*, and also a lawyer. He was deeply involved with the underground movement, and vowed to never leave his country. He spoke with passion, but, of course, in a public setting there could be no political discussions or comments that could be construed as counter-revolutionary.

I did not know how to interpret what was going on. He was just a good friend, and Mima was determine to keep it that way, although her feelings for him were visible no matter how hard she tried to hide them. This man whom she had fallen for was married. He had a very nice wife and many sons – some of whom were, at one time or another, Mima's students. Once, we visited them at their beach house, and *mi hermana* and I had a great time with his sons, who dove into the water to find starfish, seahorses, and conchs for us. Mima did not want to be responsible for breaking up his marriage. However, the temptation to spend hours talking was too much, and the two of them indulged in long conversations while they were both conscious that it could not go any farther.

One night, Mima told me years later, he came to our house after Ota, *mi hermana* and I had gone to sleep. He had been drinking and he wanted Mima to know that he loved her. He wanted to take their relationship farther, although he knew it was wrong.

Mima told him she could not become his mistress; it was against her religion and her ethics, and she had to think about her two girls.

He left. Mima told me that turning him away that night was one of the most difficult things she had done in her life.

I know Mima would have never forgiven herself had she ignored the moral principles that she held so dear. I know that her religious beliefs provided her with strength and guidance. I also know that she was human and if there was a time for her to yield to temptation, this was the time. Deep in my heart I'm convinced that it was not her faith or the moral implications – strong as they were - that kept her from getting involved. It was *mi hermana* and me. The Spanish cultural mores that formed the pillars of Cuban society would ostracize and shun us forever – a condition Mima might have been able to accept for herself, but not for her daughters.

He continued to be the love of her life, but at a distance, and in one way or another, primarily through Cuca, Mima always knew his whereabouts and his situation until he died in Miami many years later.

Chapter Fourteen

Resolution

A YEAR AFTER THE Bay of Pigs invasion, the suffocating climate of the revolution finally prompted Mima into action:

> *The academic year 61-62 developed quietly and orderly. The students had never been so disciplined. So many people had been put into prison, so many had been killed, that the students, the same as everybody else, were afraid of the ones sitting beside them. The net of espionage covered everywhere. I started to make up my mind about leaving the country.*
>
> *In that summer of 1962 I was told to teach a group of basic secondary teachers a summer course in math. It was a nice group and we enjoyed it without ever talking of politics. But now my mind was made up. I was going to leave the country that very same year. Everything was completely controlled by the government. There was not any personal freedom. I didn't want my girls to grow up*

with such rigid controls. I wanted them free, so I had to leave.

"Zeida, wherever you go, I'll follow," Ota said.

"Think about it, *Mamá*. It will not be easy." Mima worried that Ota, at her advanced age and with her unyielding character, would not be able to adjust. Besides, as long as she remained in Cuba, Ota could hold onto the hope of recovering her properties. With these properties she had rescued her family from the depths of poverty after the Great Depression. They would not be easy for her to leave behind. "You might want to move back to Cienfuegos and stay at Mamatita's house," Mima suggested, but Ota was resolute. "No, no, no, Zeida, my place is with you now." She added, echoing the sentiments of every Cuban exile: "Maybe some day we'll come back to claim what belongs to us."

Mima also asked *Abuela* Mami, but she said no. She had obligations in Cuba. One of her sisters had recently moved in and depended on her in every way. "Zeida, you've made the right decision," she told Mima. "Cuba is no longer a good place for you and the girls." She added, "I only wish my son and my other grandchildren would do the same."

What Mima called the-unknown-future-ahead-of-us, I called an adventure, and with her at my side, I was eager to face any new challenges that awaited us. The US, I imagined, must be heavenly, since most everyone we knew had sacrificed everything to get there. In contrast, Cuba was giving us a glimpse of what hell might be like. In my simplistic religious framework the players had permanently settled into their camps. Fidel personified Lucifer. He had fallen from grace and the new Cuba was his kingdom, as suffering spread throughout the land. In this place of torment, we felt deserted. I could not think of anything I would miss, except for our dog Rondy and our summer vacations in Varadero.

Chapter Fifteen

Echoes of Varadero

THERE WAS ONE DISTINCT benefit to having Ota as a grandmother. Every year she treated Mima, *mi hermana* and me to a month-long summer vacation at the beach in Varadero. For years, we had been the loyal patrons of a modest hotel located only two blocks from the beach - the unpretentious Hotel Torres. It was a friendly place and our accommodations were predictable. Ota always asked for room number three on the second floor and the owner, *Señor* Torres, made sure we always got it. The room was simple but spacious, with a small private bathroom, one large bed that *mi hermana* and I shared, and two single beds for Ota and Mima.

Every summer we had followed a rigorous routine to ensure maximum optimization of every delightful moment. In the mornings, we went to the park to ride bikes and play with other children. Then we headed to the beach. We returned to the hotel for lunch and an afternoon siesta, then went back to the beach. If the weather was not ideal, or we came back from the beach early, we visited the luxury hotels in the area – our favorite was the Oasis. In the evenings we often took a walk to the ice cream parlor, played games with our newly harvested but indispensable playmates, and listened to musicians playing in the streets.

Once in a while, we went on a horse-drawn carriage ride past the grand mansions in the area. One belonged to Batista, the ruthless dictator, and not far from it, there was a large estate that belonged to the powerful Dupont family from the US.

But the most spectacular aspect of Varadero was the beach. The water, clear as glass, provided a window to schools of fish that dashed around nervously in perfect unison. Foot-long silver fish kissed our legs. Mima said they were looking for the air bubbles forming around our skin. The sand massaged our feet as an exclusive spa never could. In the morning the beach was rarely calm, and sometimes we had to wait until the more powerful waves subsided before Mima let us go into the water. The strong surf was good, Mima said, because the breathtaking beauty of Varadero was partly due to waves that prevented algae from growing in the water. How I loved to tackle the waves at Varadero! Mima did too. She was often right there with us, while most adults sat and talked, and waited for calmer waters.

In the afternoon, vendors walked the beach, bellowing at the water's edge:

"Pirulí! Pirulí! Come and get your pirulí!"

"Mamoncillos! Mamoncillos!"

Ota treated us to the snack of our choice, which we often dunked in the salt water for an additional tasty kick.

Our vacations in Varadero taught me that it is possible, indeed preferable, to take a break from the toils of daily life without resorting to extreme luxury.

The beautiful, upscale Oasis Hotel was not far from Hotel Torres. The main attraction for *mi hermana* and me was a pool filled with colorful tropical fish, with carefully laid out stepping stones so people could walk from one end to the other. *Mi hermana* and I could spend an hour there, fooling around and jumping stones. Sometimes we hopped on one leg or, daringly, we jumped over a stone. One day the inevitable happened: the two of us fell in the water as we grabbed each other to regain our balance. I was certain that, in a matter of moments, I'd be eaten by creatures lurking in the water. Our screams pierced the serene air and disrupted the sophisticated ambience of the hotel. Mima recognized the sound of her two young cherubs. She immediately ran to our rescue and pulled us out of the fish pool.

I continued to scream. "Mima, Mima, quickly remove my tennis shoe! A fish is inside!"

She removed my sneakers. "See, there is nothing there. It's Okay."

With my hands in my crotch, I shouted, "Inside my panties! There is something inside my panties!!"

"Impossible. You were in the water for two seconds, Marina. The fish were more frightened than you were. Nothing came near you."

Her impeccable logic worked as usual. There was no stowaway fish close to my body. I was just dripping wet.

A hotel attendant brought us a couple of towels and Mima removed our clothes on the spot, while *mi hermana* and I crumpled with embarrassment. Mima laid our clothes out to dry on the grass where everyone could see them - our panties, our socks, our tennis shoes. *Mi hermana* and I sat on a bench wrapped in towels, totally humiliated. We did not return to the Oasis for days.

Sometimes, walking to the Oasis, I'd ask Mima why we did not stay there. Why did we always have to stay at the much more ordinary Hotel Torres? Her answer depended on her mood.

"Why would we want to stay there if we can go and visit anytime we want?"

Or: "Well, if we stay at the Oasis, we'll have to shorten our vacation in Varadero in half since it is twice as expensive."

Or: "The beach is nicer by us. I prefer to walk two blocks to a nicer beach than to be right on a not-so-nice beachfront."

Or: "The people at Hotel Torres are not so stuffy. We have a lot more fun there. Besides, we could not ask for a better location. The park is right next to our hotel."

I could not argue against her reasoning. I did not want our vacation shortened and I did not want to settle for a lesser beach.

It was at the park in Varadero that Mima taught us how to ride a bike, not a small feat for a woman who could not ride one herself. During our first vacation there in 1958, she decided to teach *mi hermana* to ride. She was instructed at the bike rental shop that it was simple: all she had to do was to run behind the bicycle to stabilize the seat until she could let go. In the park I looped around on my tricycle and watched the quest for mastery begin for *mi hermana*. It was evident from the outset that the bike shop had left out a few important details, so my mother, with one hand firmly planted on the handle bar and the other one on the seat, reassured *mi hermana* that she would not let her fall. Signs of progress were slow as I watched the bike wobble uncontrollably from side to side. *Mi hermana* was more than ready to abort the mission while Mima remained persuasive and persistent. "You are doing better, Zeida María. It is only a matter of practice."

After many trials, the two of them together found the rhythm of the bike, and the bike, in turn, learned to move in a straight line. I applauded that glorious moment when *mi hermana* looked back to find my mother in the distance, and realized that she, not Mima, was in control of the bike.

The following year Mima put me through a similar drill and I, like *mi hermana*, survived.

Nobody was more proud to see us riding bikes than Mima. She felt a deep sense of accomplishment in being able to help us master a skill she did not possess. And so the next year, during the summer of 1960, she decided that if she could teach us to ride a bike, she could also teach herself. So against her mother's advice and her daughters' pleas, Mima rented a bike and set out to ride it.

On a few mornings, when *mi hermana* and I arrived in the park with Ota, Mima was already out on her rented bicycle, attempting to defy the laws of gravity. She always started early, as the likelihood of crashing into an innocent soul at that time was far more remote. *Mi hermana* and I tried to keep our distance - ashamed of our own mother - but there was no good way to completely avoid her, especially when we heard, "Zeida

María! Marina! Come hold the bike for a moment just to help me get started!"

Ota, sitting alone on a shaded bench with a frown on her face, muttered, "She is going to kill herself…How does she come up with such ideas? Imagine getting on a bike…Bikes are for kids, not for a respectable woman! What kind of example is she setting for her own children?"

In Ota's world, respectable women were expected to behave in a ladylike manner at all times. They were to maintain a fair complexion by avoiding contact with the sun. Sports were off limits. An athletic physique was deemed unattractive and sweating was unbecoming. And there Mima was, the only adult on a bike, out of control, with band-aids on her elbows and knees, trying to keep her balance while everyone stayed clear of her path.

I could hear parents tell their children, "Stay away from that woman. She doesn't know what she is doing."

"*Ay Dios mío!* That woman is crazy!"

However, by the end of the summer, people praised her accomplishment, and *mi hermana* and I were proud to ride with her. Ota, however, was never pleased to watch what she called "a spectacle."

Our last trip to Varadero was for two weeks during the summer of 1962 – right after Mima decided we would leave Cuba:

Since no money could be taken out of the country I decided to spend my savings going to the hotel on the beach of Varadero.

When I finished the course for basic secondary teachers, we packed our things and were ready to leave.

That morning [my mother-in-law] came ... to say goodbye, and she told me, "Zeida, turn the radio on, as they are giving some news that may affect your trip."

I did, and I found out that the [currency] was going to be changed. New bills with different pictures and signatures would substitute for the old bills. The old ones would have no value at all in two days.

I decided I was going to go [to Varadero] anyways, and afterwards I would see what to do. When I got to the beach I learned that the money that was in the bank would be changed automatically up to $10,000. If there was more, it was lost. The money you had in cash you could change up to $600. The hotel would not accept payment in the old money, so I decided to come back to Camagüey the next day.

I left my mother and the girls at the hotel and a friend of mine that was at the same hotel, and had already changed her money, loaned me about $10 to pay the ticket for the bus and any extra that could occur. The buses were crowded and two or three times we were stopped by the militia and searched. They were always surprised to see that I had both [currencies] and each time I had to explain that I was going to Camagüey to change my old money and that I had to borrow some money from *a friend to pay for the ticket. They always allowed me to continue my trip.*

When I arrived in Camagüey, I changed some $400 that I had with me for the stay at the beach and some $200 that I had hidden at home. About the money in the bank, it was not enough as to worry me, but some people had more than $10,000 in the bank or more than $600 in cash and lost it. ... The reason is that as the banks had been nationalized people didn't trust them and some persons had thousands of dollars hidden in their houses. I think that was the main reason for the change of the money.

Mi hermana and I were so relieved when Mima returned to us in Varadero. We knew how treacherous government orders could become, so it was difficult to enjoy the beach when we were worried that Mima might get in trouble and we would never see her again.

Although we had fun, our vacation was not as fabulous as previous years. The hotel had been nationalized and *Señor* Torres was no longer in charge. This meant that we did not get our coveted room number three. Instead, we had a much smaller and noisier room on the first floor. *Señor* Torres' welcoming smile was gone, and with it, the comfortable, carefree ambience of the hotel. He was still there, but he stayed mostly in the administrative office, and the few times that we saw him, he looked serious and detached. Once, he heard Mima ask the waiter if he could bring milk for *mi hermana* and me. The waiter said there was no milk available, but then he brought two green plastic glasses full to the rim with milk, compliments of *Señor* Torres.

Mima told us that under no circumstances were we to talk about our plans to leave the country. She warned us to watch what we said at the beach, at the park, and particularly, at the hotel. This time we did not visit the Oasis. I sensed Mima did not want to walk by the militia that now guarded the hotel entrance.

But the beach was as pristine as ever. We could still build sand castles, and bathe in the crystal clear waters. We could still tackle those waves. None of these activities had yet been forbidden to Cubans. Every once in a while, Mima would whisper, "Enjoy the beach. We will not find a beach like this elsewhere."

I did not truly understand Mima's assertion that Varadero's beauty was unique. Clearly, we would find other places just as beautiful in the US. "Mima, how about Miami Beach?"

"Oh, it is not nearly as beautiful. Besides, only rich people can vacation there."

Chapter Sixteen

Preparing to Leave

WHEN [WE] CAME BACK to Camagüey, I gave final exams
to the students who had failed for the year. In Cuba, the
students who had failed had the chance to take a final
exam in September and that is why the academic year
was not considered finished until these exams were given.
After my exams and marks were done I presented my
resignation to the Director of the school. This was the first
step in order to leave the country, as they wouldn't give
you permission to leave if you still held a job.

The Director of the school at that time was a young
woman who had been my student some time ago. She
didn't have any degree from any university, but the times
when that was a requirement were over. She accepted my
resignation with tears in her eyes.

Mima's English had gotten rusty since the days when she
and Papi attended summer courses at Columbia University in
New York City. So she sought out Mr Kezar, a Canadian man

who secretly taught English in his home, and scheduled practice sessions with him twice a week.

She also had her university degrees photocopied. This was standard practice for all certified professionals leaving the country, since the originals had to remain behind.

From *Tío*, Cuca, and others in the US, Mima knew life would be difficult in the States. Cubans lawyers, physicians, accountants, businessmen and teachers were doing menial work while improving their language skills and seeking professional certification on the side. *Tío* was struggling to provide for his family. He spoke fluent English, but had no university credentials, and was no longer a young man. The entire family - *Tío*, *Tía* and Bichi - had to work to barely make ends meet. *Tío* worked at a hotel washing dishes. Bichi delivered newspapers before school and made money doing errands. *Tía* worked in a factory. Initially, the girlish stay-at-home housewife, who in Cuba spent her time creating new flower arrangements, had worked in a field picking tomatoes.

I can only imagine the anxieties lurking in Mima's mind. The responsibility to earn enough money to support Ota, *mi hermana* and me rested on her shoulders alone. In the early 1960s, Spanish was truly a foreign language in the US. Nothing was translated. She would be starting anew in her forties - a middle-aged woman in a man's world, and a foreign one at that.

Soon after our return from the beach, Mima asked *mi hermana* and me, "What do you girls think about going to Miami ahead of me? Aunt Concha wrote to me and said you could stay with her while Ota and I wait for our visa waivers."

Mima was considering sending us via Operation Pedro Pan. Concha and her daughter Marta were already taking care of Pepito's three children, and one of Marta's cousins. *Mi hermana* and I would add two more to an already overflowing pot. But for just a couple of months, Mima thought it might be fine.

I was horrified by the idea. "I'm not going anywhere without you, Mima." Separation from my mother would feel worse than losing a limb.

"Why would we need to leave without you?" *Mi hermana* asked.

"If you go now, you'll be able to start school in Miami at the beginning of the school year and it will be much easier than catching up after classes start. Besides, I'd rather you did not attend school here. You'll be subjected to indoctrination and won't learn anything of value."

I was devastated. I knew from experience that when the reason had to do with school, we were doomed. In my family, all decisions put schooling first and foremost. Pleading would do no good. We were practically on our way.

I kept thinking about Concha. Clearly, she did not know what she was offering. She had probably only seen us at our best behavior and mistakenly thought we were delightful. She, like Ota and the rest of their siblings, subscribed to the children-are-meant-to-be-seen-and-not-heard philosophy. What would she do to us?

Luckily, we never found out. Nobody was more surprised than I when, a few days later, Mima said, "I declined Concha's offer. Whatever the future holds, for better or for worse, we will stay together as a family."

We were too young to be sent away by ourselves, she said. What if something went wrong?

Phew! *Mi hermana* and I could breathe again.

We started the school year in the government-run schools since attendance was mandatory. We did not mind; our departure was imminent. All factors indicated that within a month, we would be celebrating with friends and relatives in Miami.

I already had the Visa waivers and the money orders in American money to pay for the plane tickets. My brother had sent them to us. Now they would put us on a list and let us know when our turn came. All our furniture, properties, and money would become property of the government.

For each few street blocks there was a group of people paid to [denounce] any neighbor who seemed to be selling or giving away a radio, TV set or any piece of furniture. I anyway managed to give some of my belongings to people who had been good to me. I think that everybody did, to some extent. When I was ready to leave, only waiting for my turn to come, the missile crisis occurred.

Chapter Seventeen

Cuban Missile Crisis

FROM OUR HOME IN Camagüey we followed the showdown between the US and the Soviet Union staged on Cuban soil.

In October 1962, high-flying US planes detected a build-up of approximately thirty to thirty-five Soviet missiles in Cuba aimed at the US and further missile sites under construction. President Kennedy addressed the nation and the world with a speech that identified the threat and announced a naval blockade of Cuba to prevent additional offensive weapons from reaching the island. He demanded the Soviet Union withdraw existing missiles and bombers from Cuba to avoid a nuclear confrontation.

The official news in Cuba revolved around the US threat to Cuban sovereignty and its demands to disarm Cuba, thus preventing the country from defending itself against US tyranny. The Cuban press did not offer much substance on the conflict. Cubans who wanted to be informed during these stressful and uncertain times resorted to an illegal activity - tuning shortwave radios to hear the Voice Of America

(VOA) broadcast from New York. Word from the Cuban exile community in Miami indicated that the US would surely intervene this time. There was no doubt. Indeed, listening to Kennedy's speech on the VOA broadcast, it was natural to think that the situation in Cuba was about to change. The thought that intervention might come in the form of total destruction of the island was unsettling, to say the least, but most of the counter-revolutionary community in Cuba trusted that the US would not resort to such drastic measures. Despite the recent animosity between the two countries, the embracing of Cuban refugees in Miami was evidence that a strong bond still existed between the US and Cuba. The US would not crush our island nation.

We dusted off Ota's old shortwave radio and listened to the VOA broadcast every night. The radio was moved into the living room to improve reception, although it was hidden behind a wall to conceal it from anyone entering our home, since it was counter-revolutionary to even own a shortwave radio. Every night in the darkness, we closed the doors to the balcony so that the sound would not travel to the street. The broadcast was speckled with noise, making it difficult to understand, but we sat quietly and listened attentively. One of our neighbors came and listened with us. He did not want to be seen coming to our place late at night for fear that the CDR might become suspicious, so he went up on the rooftop of his house, stepped over the division onto our rooftop and descended the spiral staircase into our back patio. The adults listened as the crisis unfolded. Afterward, they talked softly and speculated. Castro's time was over, that was certain…the US would take control… perhaps we would not need to leave Cuba after all.

Our neighbor was a very nervous young man who had recently married and, due to the housing shortage, he and his wife lived at his parents' home next door. The family was trustworthy. The parents were the former owners of the corner store where we regularly bought our groceries. In the midst of food shortages, our neighbor would inform us of incoming shipments so that we could go to the store early before the food ran out. Mima always appreciated their help. She knew how difficult it was for the older couple, who had built the family business, to now work for the government.

In the middle of the night, we listened together as the drama played out between the US and the Soviet Union. We were not alone. The world watched anxiously as the threat of a Third World War materialized in front of their eyes. The anti-Castro Cubans watched for another glimpse of hope for a free Cuba. All Cubans, regardless of political persuasion, watched as their country was used to test the balance of power.

By the end of October, three significant events had occurred: the Soviet Union agreed to dismantle their nuclear sites in Cuba on condition that the US did not threaten Cuban sovereignty. Ota's old shortwave radio finally broke down, never to be used again. And the Pan American flights from Cuba to Miami, suspended by Castro at the outset of the missile crisis, were not resumed, thus destroying our chances to leave the country:

Here I was, with my two girls and my mother, without a job and without enough savings to survive for a long

time. In order to take my job again I had to give up the
intent to leave the country, and that, I had not given up.

Roughly 1,500 Cubans had been leaving the country every week when the US-Cuba flights were discontinued. Cubans from all sectors of society, including the working class, took advantage of these flights. The main exceptions were Cubans in rural areas. Many had benefited from the Agrarian Reform. But many other small farmers could not fathom deserting the land that had been in their families for generations, even if that land was technically no longer theirs. Besides, what type of work could they do in the US?

Approximately 300,000 Cubans had left the country since 1959, injecting themselves into the bloodstream of a small, bewildered town called Miami. About 14,000 of these were children who'd entered through Operation Pedro Pan and were now unable to reunite with their parents still in Cuba. *Mi hermana* and I could have been two of these unfortunate children. How lucky for us that Mima had the foresight not to part with us! She was right: whatever hardships came our way, we were better off facing them together.

Chapter Eighteen

Haciendo la Cola

ONE DAY I DECIDED to help our food situation by hatching an egg. What better way was there to secure a steady supply of eggs than having our own egg-laying hen? I asked Mima how a hen managed such a feat and she told me that the hen kept the eggs nice and warm until they hatched. It was summer, the height of the sauna climate in Cuba, perfect for hatching eggs, I thought. I took an egg from the refrigerator and put it under a pillow in Bichi's empty bedroom. Then I proceeded to check on it four or five times every ten minutes. I'd look, tap it gently and cover it again. Sometimes I'd shake it and put it next to my ear, trying to listen to what was going on inside. That anyone would notice the egg missing from the refrigerator was the farthest thing from my mind, but in those times of food shortages, Ota kept a very close eye on our food inventory, and she noticed. I heard her agitated voice from a distance. "Who took an egg from the refrigerator? There were four eggs and now there are only three."

"*Mamá*, are you sure there were four?" Mima asked.

"There were four, all right. I had saved them for lunch today."

In the meantime, I kept going into Bichi's old room and inspecting my hidden treasure. How surprised everyone would be when I produced a chick! At lunch that day, Ota put three hard boiled eggs in front of *mi hermana* and me. She was upset and continued to talk about her missing egg. "Somebody took an egg from the refrigerator, so you'll have to split the third one between the two of you."

I started to feel bad about the whole situation, but I still hoped it would soon be forgotten. "I don't want the egg," I said.

"What? You don't like eggs? That's impossible! You are a growing child. You are not leaving the table until you have at least one." Ota responded.

"I'm not hungry!" I walked away.

Later, Ota told Mima, "Zeida, I think the maid took the egg. If she is stealing from us we have to let her go."

"I don't believe that's the case, *Mamá*," Mima said. "From what I've seen of her, she is trustworthy, and unless there is a good reason to believe that she actually took an egg from the refrigerator, we are not going to let her go."

By this time, Ota had managed to get everyone upset, particularly me. Also, my egg did not show any signs of hatching and I was concerned that someone might accidentally rest their head on Bichi's pillow and crush it. It would be pretty messy.

Ota was guarding the refrigerator like a hawk, so I could not very easily put it back. It was time to own up to my actions, so I told Mima. She sighed. She was accustomed to my silliness, but she was firm. "Marina, never, ever, take food from the refrigerator again unless Ota knows about it. Food is in short supply and we need to manage it well. The maid almost got fired because of your actions."

"But Mima, I want to put it back, but I don't want her to know. She'll be very mad at me."

"I'll call her and you put the egg back in the refrigerator. You don't have to say a word about what happened."

I did as she said. Minutes later I heard Ota say, "Where did this egg come from? Who put it here?"

Mima acted surprised. "The egg reappeared? *Mamá*, let's just accept that whoever took the egg has returned it and let's not talk about it anymore."

But Ota could not help it. She grumbled, "The things that happen in this house don't happen anywhere else…I know they don't happen by themselves… I bet the girls were involved…It was probably Zeida María. Marina is too young to do this…"

The maid was exonerated, and for now, her job was safe.

Food, especially meat, was becoming scarcer, so it was with great excitement that one day Ota came rushing into Mima's room and said, "Zeida, the meat market is open tomorrow. I just heard the news on the radio. Only one piece of meat will be allowed per customer." Then she said, "I plan to be there early in the morning, before the market opens."

Mima thought about it for a moment. "*Mamá*, you better stay home and I will go to the market."

"No, no, no, no, no." In Cuban dialect, or perhaps just in my family, a single "no" leaves the door open for further negotiation. Multiple "nos" let people know that you really mean it. "You have other things to do. I'll do it. I'll take one of the small children's chairs with me and I'll just sit in line until the market opens. We have to get meat for these girls. At their age they need protein."

The mental image of Ota sitting in a child's chair was comical. Ota was diabetic and heavy. She had no physical endurance whatsoever. At 66, it was difficult for her to walk at a normal pace or to stand for long periods of time without becoming incapacitated due to exhaustion or a blood sugar crisis. Consequently, Ota rarely ventured outside the home. But her mind was much stronger than her body and she was determined to be the one to get food on the table.

Next morning, when *Abuela* Mami dropped off our bread for breakfast, she saw *la cola* – the line - at the market, wrapping around the block. Later in the morning Ota came home, looking defeated.

"*Mamá*, what happened?" Mima asked.

"Oh Zeida, it was terrible. I sat in *la cola* at the crack of dawn this morning until the market opened. But when *la cola* started moving, I had a cramp and I could not get out of the chair, so everyone just went around me. Nobody bothered to help me!"

"Ay Mamá..."

"It was a mob! The moment the market opened, everyone pushed and shoved their way in. I could not get near the place and I did not know what to do with the chair once I got up."

"Well, you did what you could do. At least you did not get hurt."

That evening at the dinner table, while eating a typical meal – rice, beans, possibly with a piece of pork rind, and bananas - we talked about Ota's outing. She was devastated. *Mi hermana* and I were amused. Mima was concerned, and *Abuela* Mami, who regularly joined us for dinner, was pensive. She was older than Ota, but in much better physical condition. She said, "Next time it's my turn. I will do *la cola* and get the meat."

A few weeks later, *Abuela* Mami brought home a pound of beef. Ota was ecstatic as she planned the evening meal. She decided to freeze half of it for another day. Knowing how much *mi hermana* liked thin steaks, breaded and lightly fried – *Bistec de Palomilla* - Ota told the maid to slice the meat into very thin steaks. It had gristle and looked tough, so after it was sliced, each piece was pounded and salted to tenderize it and then, since there were no eggs, Ota used a bit of milk mixed with water to dip the steaks before breading. The next trick was to find some fat to fry them in. There was no oil or butter, but Ota had a bit of lard that she valued more than gold. She brought it out from its secret compartment and used barely enough to cover the bottom of the frying pan. Any grease left over from frying the steaks was refrigerated. It could be used the next day to add meat flavor to the beans.

That evening, for the first time in weeks, we ate meat. Ota proudly served *mi hermana* and me and then she served *Abuela* Mami, who refused. Rice and beans were enough for her, she said. Mima waited to see if *mi hermana* and I wanted seconds. Ota gave part of her piece to the maid and left the other just in case we might want more. After we finished our pieces, the adults shared the remains. What a meal! Ota was already thinking about how to cook the other half of the meat, which she planned to serve a week later.

Some time after this, there was news that chickens would be available at the meat market, one chicken per family. This was more exciting than winning the lottery, since chicken had become a delicacy of extreme proportions. Mima and *Abuela* Mami took turns *haciendo la cola*, and finally, Mima appeared at our door with a brown bag with holes in it…the chicken was alive.

Mima did not know what to do. She took it to the back patio and tied it to a railing and closed the door to prevent our beagle-type-mutt Rondy from attacking the frightened bird.

She knew she would also need to handle the situation with me.

I had always been fascinated by the animal kingdom. I often entertained myself with bugs and other critters. I liked to load my bubble-gum-colored rubber truck with ants from a colony in the back patio and introduce them to another colony on the balcony. I convinced myself that I was helping them get to know each other better, or perhaps I reduced their travel time, since I often saw a pilgrimage of ants traveling through the hallway. It was likely that they visited their relatives in the other colonies in the same way we visited our relatives in Cienfuegos. I also succeeded in broadening the horizon of lizards, those shy creatures that preferred to camouflage in their surroundings. I took them to places where they could showcase their magnificent vibrant colors. Just like us, I figured they could use a change in scenery, and I was there to make it happen. I attempted similar arrangements with crickets, although they often jumped out of my truck, never to be seen again.

I gained a lot of satisfaction from being nature's helper. It was no secret that I yearned for chickens and fluffy little baby chicks, horses and cows. I wanted to live on a farm, not just visit one. I liked Castro's proposal for a new breed of cows small enough for every family to keep their own and produce milk, even in the city. Everyone we knew thought it was a ridiculous idea, but not me. I was ready to pamper our very own cow, which would live on our rooftop. The logistics on how to get a sizable animal to climb the spiral staircase to the rooftop never entered my mind. Fortunately for my mother, the opportunity never materialized, but I was always on the lookout for more pets. Rondy was not enough.

I said, "Mima, can we keep the chicken for a pet?"

"Don't get any ideas. This chicken is not a pet. It is our food. We will kill it and eat it."

I could not believe that these words were coming from my loving mother. "Mima, you can't do this. It would be sooo cruel. Perhaps she can lay eggs and we can eat those!"

"No Marina, this chicken will not yield eggs. I know this decision is difficult for you to accept, but these are the facts."

"Mima, if you kill the poor bird I won't eat. Please, let's keeeeppppp heeerrr…."

I was convinced that my mother could not carry out such an act no matter what she said, so I set out to find a proper name for my new pet.

Meanwhile, Mima pondered how to convert this living creature into food. She asked the maid if she knew how to kill the animal. She said that she had never killed a chicken.

However, she would be happy to prepare the chicken after it had been killed. Ota could not kill a chicken.

Mima decided she was the only one who could do it. She considered her options. She could cut off its head with a big kitchen knife, but she was afraid she might hurt herself in the process. It would be messy. As a youngster in Spain, she vaguely remembered watching the tortured death of a chicken, when an incision was made on its head and the animal was bled. She knew she could not do that.

She had heard about the method of holding the chicken by the head and twirling it around to break its neck. No knives, no blood. This sounded like the best alternative. She would do it early next morning before anyone was awake.

In the early morning hours, before *Abuela* Mami dropped off our morning bread, Mima got out of bed, went to the patio, grabbed the chicken by the head and with her arm extended as far from her body as possible and her eyes tightly shut, she violently twirled the animal around over and over again, until it felt limp in her hand. She left the bird on the kitchen counter for the maid to prepare upon her arrival. My mother had killed so we could eat.

When I woke up, I immediately went to the patio. I had thought of a name for my new pet. She would be called Rosalinda, after a beautiful girl in a storybook. I pictured myself every morning getting fresh eggs from Rosalinda. We would be able to eat rice and fried eggs for lunch – one of my favorite dishes. I had to talk with Mima about getting grain for her to eat. We would also need to get some hay – she needed a nice cushiony surface for her eggs.

But a few white feathers were the only trace of Rosalinda that I found in the patio. I could hear a lot of commotion in the kitchen. I peeked in cautiously, for this was Ota's domain and she did not allow children to enter. I was shocked by what I saw. The maid was plucking my bird. I ran to Mima in despair, "Mima, Ota killed Rosalinda!" I knew that Ota was behind all evil doings in our home.

"No, Marina. Ota did not kill the chicken. I did. I told you that the chicken was our food."

"You did it? How could you! How can you be so cruel?"

I thought my mother was incapable of inflicting harm on a living creature. Now I had to re-assess her character.

That evening, we had chicken fricassee for dinner. Ota served me a drumstick, knowing how much I liked the dark meat. I looked at it and asked, "Is this Rosalinda?"

Mima nodded. The drumstick seemed to take on a different character. I had never associated eating meat with a living creature. I left the table in distress. I later had some rice with a little fricassee sauce.

Thanks to Ota's creativity in the kitchen, Rosalinda was dinner for many days - chicken croquettes, chicken meatballs, chicken soup and chicken giblets in sauce. It was impossible not to eat for so many days. After going hungry the first day, I began to eat and tried not to think of my would-be pet, and nobody used the word "chicken" when talking about food.

"What are we having for dinner?" I would ask.

"Croquettes," or "soup," or "rice with liver" was the response. Even Rosalinda's bones became a source of nourishment, as we broke each bone and gnawed on them like dogs.

Rationing of food, shoes, and clothing was instituted in March of 1962. Every family received a handwritten card from the CDR with the names of each family member and their monthly allotment of goods. At the time, rationing was a welcomed idea since it set expectations and could potentially eliminate the food lines. But this was not the case. *Haciendo la cola* to buy goods became the norm:

> *About food, there was less in the store than what you were allowed to buy. I remember once that for a full week we didn't have anything to eat but lentils. Every evening my mother and I would clean them of small stones and dirt in order to cook them next day.*

The beans, whichever type was available, were dirty with sand, stones and dead bugs. Mima and Ota stayed up late, sorting the beans from the debris, before soaking them over night. Ota would go through the beans once and then Mima would go through them a second time since Ota's sight prevented her from doing a thorough job. *Mi hermana* and I occasionally relieved Ota when her eyes got tired, but we really lacked the patience required to do it right, and Mima often had to screen them again.

Haciendo la cola consumed a significant portion of every able adult's time, and it became a way of life for generations to come - not just for food, but for such necessities as clothing fabric and shoes. While in other parts of the world people could spend time doing something useful with their lives, we

Cubans - that is, Cubans who did not hold important positions within the revolutionary government - stood in *colas*:

> *Food and clothing had never been expensive in my country, and now they were so scarce that even having the money you could not buy them. My girls were growing and needed bigger clothes. It was impossible to buy new ones because there were no materials. I made skirts and blouses from the skirts of the old dresses. With shoes it was a different story. No one can stretch out shoes. There were no shoes in the shoe stores. I mean, there were, but in the windows, not to be sold. Each family had a notebook where they wrote down anything you bought and there was some amount that was the maximum you could buy. About shoes, it was two pairs of shoes a year per person. But there were no shoes.*

Mima went to see the cobbler, a man who now was busier than ever fixing old shoes. Perhaps he would know if there was a way to buy second-hand shoes.

"What many people are doing with the shoes of growing kids," he said, "is that they are cutting off the tip to make room for the toes. If you bring the shoes, I can open the toe."

And so we and other youngsters had open-toe shoes. This was at least an interim solution until we could get new ones.

Fortunately for us, *mi hermana* and I had a good friend whose parents had been the owners of a shoe store, and while the store now belonged to the government, they were still in charge of the day-to-day operations. From time to time, Janet's mother would tell Mima, "Zeida, we are getting a new shipment tomorrow. What size are the girls so I can try to save them a pair?" Sometimes we went to the store the night before so she could measure our feet. "I'll try to hide a pair for each of them," she would say, "but come early because I don't know what I'll be able to do."

Next day, we were in *la cola* just like everyone else. Once in the store, we were pretty certain to get the correct size. If none of the government agents were watching, Janet's mother would not even mark our rationing card, but sometimes she had no choice. Of course, Janet's mother could only help when there was merchandise available, which was seldom.

Then, people started making shoes with some upholstery material that came from China and the soles were made with a piece of automobile tire. Those shoes, my girls had to wear for a long time.

For ten pesos a cobbler would trace the foot and provide the tire tread for the sole, and the customer supplied the colorful Chinese cloth.

There were no stockings, and socks were knitted at home using several strands of sewing thread. Also thin cotton rope of that kind used to tie packages in the stores. The needles were made of the spokes of old bicycles.

Once we got a good amount of wool from China and that winter the ones that didn't know how to knit learned, so they could have sweaters.

Mima taught *mi hermana* and me to knit. She even showed us how to make the ankle part of the sock – quite tricky - and we, in turn, taught many of our friends.

Christmas of 1962, the first Christmas after the Missile Crisis, brought an unexpected surprise. The US traded $53M in medical supplies and food in exchange for the Bay of Pigs prisoners. The food was mostly baby food and powdered milk, but for a few days the stores were filled with goods that had not been seen in a long time - canned peaches and Jello were some of my favorites.

In addition to shortages, we faced other problems:

The economic situation was getting harder for me... even though there was not too much on which to spend the money, some was needed to survive. Then I started tutoring kids in my home. It was very unstable work, as some students would come for 2 months, others for 15 days, others stayed with me all the time, but I didn't know if they were going to quit or not. So, every month I would wonder if I would be able to afford the expenses of the next month. Thanks to God, I always did.

Mima's tutoring was illegal, and thus, one more source of anxiety in her life. She set the rule that only two students could come into our home at the same time, and she requested that no one linger outside our door. If questioned, she and her students were prepared to say that it was only a visit to their long-time teacher. Luckily, everyone was discreet and the CDR never asked questions or in any manner acted suspicious. In a way, being right in the heart of the city, amidst all the hustle and bustle, made our home an ideal place for covert activities.

Chapter Nineteen

Christmas in Cienfuegos

THE TRADITIONAL CUBAN Christmas was firmly planted in Spanish religious customs: a nativity scene was the focal point of the season's decorations, and on January 6th children found a few presents at the foot of their beds from the Three Kings.

By the time *mi hermana* and I were born, US influence had brought Christmas trees and, of course, Santa Claus. And while some families continued to strictly observe Spanish traditions, others recognized Santa as the gift bearer. In our family, Mima made sure that the Three Kings as well as Santa thought *mi hermana* and I were special.

One of my earliest remembrances of Christmas was when we still lived in the upstairs apartment of *Abuela* Mami's house. Mima, with the help of our maid Lucía, decorated a synthetic white Christmas tree with shiny colorful ornaments while keeping an eye on *mi hermana* and me. We were eager to help, but we had been instructed in no uncertain terms to look but not touch. After the tree was decorated, I watched Mima carefully unwrap the porcelain nativity pieces and arranged them under the tree: the Three Kings, an angel, a few farm animals, Mary and Joseph, and, of course, a most endearing baby Jesus on a crate filled with hay. How I ached to hold him in my arms! But Mima would not allow it. She warned me, "Marina, you stay away from baby Jesus. He is to be admired only from afar."

Surely I was young then, but I thought, what harm could come from a soft caress, or a gentle kiss? So I kept insisting. "Mima, please, please, please, just let me kiss him. I just want to kiss baby Jesus. I promise I will not pick him up. Pleeaase, I promise I will not pick him up."

Mima could only resist my begging for so long. "Okay Marina, you can kiss him, but be very, very careful. He is delicate and fragile."

I approached baby Jesus, closed my eyes, and kissed his slightly raised infant leg, the one that gave an illusion of playful movement. To my utter amazement, the leg came off. In my mind, it had been nothing short of a miracle, an indication that I deserved to keep a part of Him. In my mother's eyes, it was a clear confirmation that I was not to be trusted around delicate porcelain figures. She took the leg from me, and said firmly, trying hard not to laugh, "See why I did not want you to touch baby Jesus?"

"But Mima, all I did was to kiss his little leg! It came off by itself. Honest!"

"Well, all I know was that baby Jesus had both of his legs before you kissed him."

Mima glued baby Jesus back together and made him look as good as new...almost. There was always a visible line at the joining of the leg.

Every year, after we decorated our tree, we traveled to Cienfuegos to spend Christmas with the rest of our family. At Oto and Ota's small apartment there were no Christmas decorations, but the Three Kings always left *mi hermana* and me a few presents at the foot of our beds. The best part was seeing Ota open the bag of coal left at the foot of her bed. *Mi hermana* and I felt vindicated. Even the Three Kings disapproved of her bad temper.

After Oto died, Ota, Mima, *mi hermana* and I stayed at Mamatita's house, the hub of all family activities, especially on Christmas Eve.

There, a spectacular nativity scene filled almost the entire living room. The pieces were small but bountiful. They recounted the story from the Annunciation, when Gabriel told the Virgin Mary that she would become the mother of Jesus, to the Nativity in Bethlehem. A continuous line of visitors dropped in to admire the beautiful display, but I was only allowed to enter the room under close supervision after Mima told my baby Jesus story.

A small altar and a real Christmas tree also graced Mamatita's living room. Yes, a real Christmas tree, probably from the US or some other distant land. It was a yearly gift from the owner of the Eureka store, who was forever grateful after Paco, Mamatita's son – Ota's brother - performed a surgery that saved his life.

In the early Christmas celebrations that I remember, Mamatita's house was filled with forty or more of her descendants, friends and relatives, many of whom traveled from faraway places to reunite as a family once a year. The talking never stopped. A year's worth of events and emotions had to gush out in just a few hours.

Two of Mamatita's five daughters, Fefa and Anita, who lived with her, toiled for days in preparation for the big feast. Throughout Christmas Eve day, the aroma of the slow-roasting pig permeated every corner of the house. Packages arrived from relatives in Spain with an assortment of *turrones,* sweet treats made of honey and nuts, and *sidra,* a sweet alcoholic sparkling cider that Mima let us sample from her glass. "This tastes better than champagne," she told us.

The conversation and laughter came to an abrupt halt when Mamatita, in her late 80s and almost blind, entered the dining room to preside over the Christmas Eve banquet. The Matriarch of the family, petit and unassuming, with a cane in one hand and her daughter Fefa by her side, commanded the respect of everyone. Her calm presence and gentle smile underscored our family unity. How fortunate we were to celebrate this moment together! Everyone took their seats after she was comfortably seated at the long table, which extended over to the patio. Paco, her only son and the family's benefactor, sat by her side, and conversation and laughter once again flooded the room over the clatter of serving utensils. The food was magnificent, but it was the overflowing affection, the memories, the stories and the jokes, enhanced by the Cuban flare for embellishment, that made these festivities the most anticipated event of the year.

It was during these gatherings that I learned about the adventures of Concha's son, Pepito, in Texas. He had traveled to King Ranch to find out more about the famous Santa Gertrudis cattle, which he hoped to import to the ranch he operated in

Cuba. When he first arrived in Texas, he went to a restaurant and could not understand the menu and, of course, he could not let the pretty waitress know that he was clueless, so he pointed to three items. She looked at him, baffled. "Are you sure? Those are three complete meals." He did not understand: in Cuba he was accustomed to ordering a la carte, so in broken English, he assured her, "Yes, of course. That's what I want."

"But…"

He was adamant. When the waitress brought out three salads, he knew he had made a terrible mistake. The three salads were followed by three complete dinners. Huge portions of food were served and he had no choice but to eat every last bite. He didn't want the waitress to think he had made an error. After all, he was representing Cuba.

A few hours later, he was the only patron left in the restaurant, still finishing his meals. He was bursting at the seams and uncertain he could stand, but he thought, if I don't order dessert, they'll surely know. So he did.

This time, he only pointed to one entry in the menu and the waitress brought a large piece of cake.

"But *oyeme*, they don't fool around with the serving portions in Texas!" he told us. He looked at the mountain of cake before him, inconspicuously loosened his belt, and downed the dessert.

He paid the bill and inched his way out of the restaurant, which was, by then, closed. He walked for a long time to aid the digestive process and never returned.

I also remember hearing about Mima's role in the romance between Panchita - Mamatita's youngest daughter – and her husband Felix.

Panchita was in danger of remaining single. All her sisters had married in their late teens or early twenties, but Panchita was almost thirty and still had no prospects for matrimony. It was not her looks – she was quite attractive. It was her personality. The traits of Ota's character were seeded in Panchita, but she also had an independent streak that made it impossible for her to accept a mere mortal for her husband.

Finding a husband for Panchita became a family priority. Her sister Anita started to invite her to a weekly dance that she attended with her husband Rafael. Eligible young men from "respectable families" would travel on horseback a considerable distance to dance with suitable young women late into the night. Of course, a chaperone made sure that proper behavior was observed at all times.

There was a particular young man, Felix, one of Rafael's friends, who stood out from the rest. At the end of the dance he did not show any signs of exhaustion, not even the slightest trace of perspiration on his beautiful tailored, neatly starched shirt. Imagine that - a man who defied the tropical heat. All the women found him enchanting. This was not hard to believe: in addition to his perfect grooming, he was tall, thin, and refined. But of all the women to choose from, it was Panchita that he wooed.

Seeing Felix's popularity with the women, a young man asked him, "Felix, how do you manage not to perspire? What is your secret? Are you not made out of flesh and blood like the rest of us?"

Felix confessed: beneath his undershirt, he placed blotting paper to absorb the perspiration. He also brought a fresh shirt so he could change during the course of the evening.

Panchita found his elegance captivating.

Felix, ever the proper gentleman, followed the established courting ritual. He visited Panchita at Mamatita's house, and later, he was allowed to take her out to the park or the movies, although they had to find a chaperone. Panchita asked if Mima, who was in her early teenage years, could take on this very serious and important responsibility. She was vigilant, no doubt a quality every chaperone resume should list. Ota agreed. And indeed, Panchita was right: Mima turned out to be the perfect chaperone. Felix and Panchita learned that she could be easily enthralled with the moving pictures, or distracted with an ice cream cone at the park, allowing the *novios* to have a little privacy.

At the end of The Christmas Eve celebration, the women and a few of the men attended midnight Mass. *Mi hermana* and I, along with the other children, tired and under the influence of the *Sidra*, would go to sleep and await Santa Claus.

Christmas was never the same after the revolution. The first Christmas under Castro was marked by the abolition of Santa Claus, a symbol of US imperialism. Subsequent Christmas celebrations at Mamatita's were attended by fewer friends and family members, as more of them left the country. We no longer had the roasting pig, the *Sidra* and the *Turrones*, although someone - probably Paco - used his connections to get a bit of pork on Christmas Eve.

Even after Mamatita died in 1963, at the age of ninety-two, we and those other family members still in Cuba continued to travel to Cienfuegos at Christmas time. Mamatita's spirit still united the family, but too many things had changed and too many concerns festered in everyone's mind to make it truly festive. The stories now centered on the tribulations of our new way of life, the adventures of those determined to test the system, and the longing for loved ones far away.

Some situations were still humorous.

One of Mima's cousins told us how she cut off the head of a live turkey on her patio, and to her surprise, the headless bird ran around her house gushing blood, as if possessed. Horrified, she grabbed her daughter and climbed on top of the dining room table, and remained there long after the bird went limp. Needless to say, dinner was not ready when her husband came home.

There were stories of those who tried to sneak jewelry and other valuables out of the country before the flights to Miami were cancelled.

A man, taken to the airport by his brother, hid jewelry within the seams of his clothes. As they parted, the brother said, "Chico, do me a favor, let me know how you make out so that I know to follow suit when my turn comes."

"How am I going to let you know?"

"Signal me with your hat. The more to the front you wear it, the more things they took from you. If your hat is all the way back, it means that you were successful. If only a few pieces of jewelry were confiscated, wear your hat straight on top. If they found everything, place your hat over your forehead. I'll watch by the window."

The man patiently waited for his brother to board the plane. After awhile, he spotted a man with a hat covering his entire face. It was his brother.

There were success stories as well. Another man decided to wear a cast on his arm, pretending it was broken. The guard said to him, "I cannot allow you on the plane with that cast on."

"But what can I do? I broke my arm yesterday and the doctor said I had to wear it."

"Well, it will have to be replaced. As far as I know, you could be using the cast to smuggle valuables and we are not going to stand for that. One of our doctors will replace it."

"Oh please, *Señor*, at least let me call my own doctor, who is acquainted with my fracture. It would be much better if he does it. Can I call him?"

"Okay. I don't care who does it, but we must replace your cast."

His doctor came and replaced the cast. The newly applied plaster contained all his jewelry.

Many conversations were devoid of humor. Pepito and his wife Yolanda related news from their visits to Paquito, Concha's other son, still in prison. They told us that Paquito had asked one of the other inmates to draw the faces of his six children on a handkerchief, using a small picture he carried as his only treasure.

Pepito was now serious and quiet, a sad contrast to the man who had once loved to tell stories. At the ranch, his thoroughbred breeding bulls had been butchered for meat, destroying a new breed of cattle he had worked so hard to develop by crossing those Santa Gertrudis bulls he had imported from King Ranch with Aberdeen cows. The militia used his chickens for target practice – no wonder Cubans were going hungry. His wife, Yolanda, kept incessantly busy to avoid thinking about her children in Miami.

Panchita and Felix talked about their daughter, Mercy, their only offspring, whom they had treated like a princess since the day she was born. She was in Miami with aunt Concha. How long before they could once again reunite and celebrate Christmas together?

What they did not know was that the day would never come.

Chapter Twenty

Hurricane Fury

IN OCTOBER OF 1963, Hurricane Flora hit Cuba, and Camagüey was right in its path. We prepared our home the best we could. We moved the patio furnishings inside, shut all the doors tightly, taped all the windows, collected water in the bathtub and in buckets, placed candles within reach, and bought alcohol to fuel the cooking contraption called *el reverbero*. Mima asked *Abuela* Mami if she wanted to stay with us, but she could not. Her sister Sara and her companion both suffered from agoraphobia and could not leave the house. They needed her.

The storm came. Within moments, the winds shook every door. Torrential rain pounded hard and loud. Everything went dark. Mima, Ota, *mi hermana* and I nestled together in the living room. No TV, no radio, no lights. We played Canasta, Dominoes, Monopoly, until it was too dark to see, all the while cuddling Rondy, whose animal sense told him this was no regular storm. *Mi hermana* and I slept with Mima - a privilege reserved only for when we were sick - and Rondy was also allowed to stay with us in the confines of her bedroom. Rondy had never, ever, been allowed to sleep with us, but his sleeping quarters could only be reached by opening the door to the back patio. Besides, how could we leave him alone? This brave little creature, the only male in our midst, trembled and clung to us for dear life. I was determined to protect him with my life, if necessary.

Mima's bedroom was our Noah's ark - solid, stable, impenetrable. There, we felt safe.

Days passed and what seemed to be the climax of the storm also passed, but the heavy rains and winds persisted. The air became oppressive, humid and hot.

Finally, the rain tapered off, and Mima gingerly opened one of the doors to the balcony. Everything seemed calm. I immediately asked Mima if I could go and check on *Abuela* Mami.

"Impossible, Marina. The streets are covered with water and there is not a soul out there. We need to stay put for now."

No doubt Mima was being overly cautious. The sky was blue, the air was crisp, and there was no detectable wind - by all accounts, a beautiful day. After so many days trapped inside the house, I was dying to get out. Besides, we had no electricity so we were completely isolated from the rest of the world. The only way to find out what was going on was to go out.

I was not worried about the water in the streets.

Before I could argue my point, the winds and rain returned, and we were once again sitting in the dark. Was it a different storm? We did not know for sure.

Again, days passed. The storm seemed even more menacing than before. Then, a frightening sound, louder than nearby thunder, rocked our ark.

Mima went on an exploration mission through darkened rooms to see what could have happened, but everything looked fine from the inside.

Mi hermana and I were running out of distractions. Mima challenged us to invent new card games to restrain us from turning on each other. *The Lord of the Flies* would not have made good reading material at this point.

Our supply of food and water was dwindling. I could see the worried look on Ota's and Mima's faces as they inventoried what was left. But I was not afraid. I was certain that Mima could resolve any problem. Besides, *mi hermana* and I could not stomach another bowl of cold beans and rice, so going hungry was not a concern we shared. Indeed, at this point, it sounded like a good alternative.

Finally, the rain subsided and Mima again opened the door to the balcony. The air, once again, was crisp. The empty streets were submerged in water. "I think this time it is really over," she said. "I'm going to go next door to see if they know what's going on." When Mima opened the door to the back patio to go up to the rooftop and cross over to the neighbor's side, there it was: the culprit of that horrible sound a few days earlier. The tall chimney from the downstairs bakery had fallen onto our back patio and huge pieces of concrete were lying everywhere. Mima let out a sigh. Had the chimney fallen at a slightly different angle, it would have destroyed our home, and us. Luckily, only the spiral staircase to the rooftop suffered severe damage.

We no longer had a TV – I'm not sure if it was broken, given away, or sold. However, we heard from our neighbor that houses close to the river were completely under water. "Ay --

Ernestina!" Mima worried about *Abuela* Mami. She lived closer to the river than we did. So as soon as it was safe to go out, Mima sent *mi hermana* and me to check on her. We were very eager to venture out after spending twelve days indoors. With water rolling down the cobblestone streets, *mi hermana* and I tried to keep our feet dry by walking single file, one foot in front of the other on the edges of the old sidewalks from colonial times that dipped in the center where the water flowed. Nevertheless, by the time we arrived at *Abuela* Mami's house, our feet were drenched.

She was so happy to see us. The water from the river had stopped climbing less than a block from her house. We told her about the chimney from the bakery, and she showed us the chairs on top of the tables where she was going to sit her sister and her companion if the water started coming into the house.

An inspector came to our house to survey the damage from the chimney. Upon careful review, he said we would have to live with the staircase as it was, but he would send someone to remove the debris.

"But where am I going to do the laundry if I don't have access to the rooftop?" asked Mima.

"*Señora*, this is the least of our worries. Believe me, you were extremely lucky. There are many others who have encountered much more serious damage."

Mima agreed.

In addition to providing an easy way to visit the neighbors, and a place for washing and hanging clothes, the rooftop was also where *mi hermana* and I played with Rondy and with our friends. Still, in contrast to the disaster around us, losing access to it was little more than an inconvenience.

Mima was no civil engineer, but she devised a way to make the staircase usable again. The damage was limited to an area of about six feet. Mima found a large piece of the wrought iron side railing among the debris from the chimney. She laid the broken railing on its side, like a ladder, and connected it to the undamaged portion of the staircase. She tried it. She said it was usable, but only by her.

From then on, Mima climbed through the damaged part of the stairway and we handed her the basket of laundry from below. After the first few weeks, she gained confidence, and let *mi hermana* and me also climb up to the rooftop. Rondy, the wonder dog, soon managed his way up to the rooftop as well, although coming down was a trickier proposition. After a precarious attempt that almost ended his life, he shied away from descending on his own. He barked until someone climbed up and carried him down. It was usually me. Rondy gladly accepted my budding motherly tendencies.

The one person never to climb the collapsed staircase was Ota, but she had never set foot on the rooftop before - the kitchen was her domain.

Shortly after the hurricane, Lucía, our faithful maid from the pre-Ota era, came to visit us. We were used to occasional visits by some of our previous maids. Sometimes they were looking for work, sometimes for help, but Lucía had not visited us since Ota's temper drove her away. Once or twice Mima had taken *mi hermana* and me on a long and tortuous bus ride to a poverty-stricken area to visit her, but we knew she could never be part of our family again.

I remember seeing her cry on the afternoon she left us. She had said to Mima:

"Zeida, I can't stay here any longer. I try to follow your mother's instructions, but she is never satisfied. Nothing I do pleases her, no matter how hard I try."

Mima was not surprised. The kitchen walls were not thick enough to contain the daily arguments and strife that took place there, but Mima felt helpless.

"I'm so sorry, Lucía. I know how difficult my mother is, but I cannot turn her away and I cannot change her."

We were all so sad, even *Abuela* Mami. Of course, *mi hermana* and I took every opportunity to vilify Ota, and to make her feel bad for what she had caused. I actually think she did feel bad; she was unusually quiet for days.

Immediately, Mima started the search for a new maid. She looked for someone who could work well under Ota's management and, at the same time, fulfill the caring role that had made Lucía such a welcome addition to our home. Finding someone with those qualifications proved as difficult as finding an honest and competent president for Cuba. Some maids only lasted a few days. Some lasted a month. Dishonesty and incompetence abounded. Compromises were made, and in the end, we settled for someone far less enjoyable than our one and only Lucía.

But Ota was not bad – she was just bad-tempered. Whenever household help dropped in, often with their children tagging along, Ota fed them. She could not stand the sight of hungry children, and she would send them home with a goody bag as well. Mima would also go through our old clothes and put together a bag for them to take.

However, times had changed, and when Lucía came to visit us, we could not help her; we could just barely take care of ourselves. Our last maid -- the one who almost got blamed for the egg I stole from the refrigerator – was no longer with us because Mima could not afford to pay her.

Lucía looked a little older, a little grayer, but she still flashed that loving smile, the one that put everyone but Ota at ease. I heard Mima say, "Ay Lucía, I wish I could offer you a job, but I can't. Not now. I'm no longer teaching, so I don't really have an income. These days I'm doing the cleaning and laundry myself. Occasionally, a woman comes in to help me in exchange for tutoring her son. I'm sorry."

"*Señora*, don't worry. If you can't pay me, that's Okay. I'll work for you for room and board only."

"But I cannot even manage that! I cannot afford to feed you."

Mima took the bread remaining from our breakfast and gave it to her. "Here. It's bread from the downstairs bakery. It's all we have."

Lucía took it. We hugged her and Mima told her to come by anytime. "Next time bring your grandson to play with the girls."

That was the last time we saw her.

Chapter Twenty-One

School, *Gusarapos,* and Fellow *Gusanos*

AFTER THE BAY OF Pigs invasion, *mi hermana*'s school teacher left the country, and her replacement was barely qualified after receiving only six weeks of training. She was able to spout the virtues of the revolution, but had problems with long division. In my family, this was not acceptable, so the search for a tutor began. *Abuela* Mami used her extensive network of teachers in Camagüey and found just what she was looking for - a retired teacher with a good reputation.

We walked to Teri's house every day for our lesson. She lived in one of those old Spanish colonial houses with *tinajones* in the garden, the large terracotta pots used to collect rain water – the symbol of the city of Camagüey. This meant one thing to *mi hermana* and me: we had to carefully inspect our drinking water to make sure it was free of *gusarapos,* the larvae that often eluded the water filtering process. Teri claimed that there was nothing wrong with *gusarapos* in the drinking water;

in fact, they consumed undesirable bacteria and algae, and helped to keep the water fresh. But *mi hermana* and I did not want to have those creepy crawlers in our bodies, so we only asked for water under extreme circumstances.

Unfortunately, the old adage that those who drink water from the *tinajones* never leave the city proved false. After we had spent a few months under Teri's tutelage, she joined the exile community in Miami, and *Abuela* Mami had to find us a new tutor.

Consuelo came to teach us at home. She did not have the same enthusiasm as Teri and there were no extras, such as hunting for *gusarapos* in our water glass. Often the tutoring sessions were drawn out and boring, so it was a relief for me when the government declared that all school age children had to attend the public schools. We were enrolled in a school that in its previous life had been a Catholic school for girls, but now was public and coed.

Academically, our first school year in the government-run school was disorganized and unsettling. *Mi hermana* was more advanced in math than her teacher, but her teacher had been Mima's student and treated *mi hermana* well. However, the majority of teachers carried a grudge against us. We were *gusanos* and often - particularly during History class, when the treachery of the elite against the struggling poor was the underlying message - the other students subjected *mi hermana* and me to long, serious stares, looks that made it clear that we were the enemy.

It was common knowledge that our mother had resigned her position so that we could leave the country. Also, Mima and *Abuela* Mami were members of the pre-Castro academic community and woven into the established academic fabric of Camagüey, now labeled an oligarchy. One of *mi hermana*'s teachers did not hesitate to mention in class that Zeida Villa and Ernestina Larrauri - *Abuela* Mami - had obtained their teaching positions not based on merit, but through connections in a corrupt system. We knew that this was not true, but the truth did not make us feel comfortable in the presence of public assertion. Thankfully, we found other *gusano* students who soon became our friends.

Our new friends were from families who lived close to the park and who had owned small businesses - a store, a diner, an inn. Many of these small merchants had dedicated their lives to building their businesses, and did not know how to break from them and start anew. They thought they could ride out the storm; they had weathered difficult times before, and Castro, they hoped, was another transitory tempest. Many of them lacked the formal education or professional credentials that would open opportunities in the US. Few, if any, could speak English. And how would they raise capital to open a new business?

One family had immigrated to Cuba from Lebanon hoping for a better life. It had taken them many years of hard work to make a decent living from their store. Another friend's parents had emigrated from Spain after the Civil War, seeking peace and stability. Through the years they had built a reputation within the community and established themselves as successful owners of an inn.

Now, these small businesses belonged to the state, although as it was with our beloved Hotel Torres in Varadero, the original owners continued to be involved in the day-to-day operations.

After the Bay of Pigs, after the Missile crisis, these middle class proprietors started to recognize that Castro's tentacles had a firm grasp, and that the prospect for change looked dim. The revolution could no longer be equated to a passing storm. It had morphed into a never-ending cataclysmic deluge. These sentiments, however, were not discussed in public, but only in the company of intimate friends and relatives.

In time, a few of our friends joined the revolutionary cause. It was the only way for them to go on living in the new Cuba.

However, most of our girlfriends managed to eventually leave the country. Some settled in Puerto Rico. One left Cuba through Mexico with her husband and young son. The three of them waded across the Río Grande into the US. Another friend was one of the 125,000 Cubans who arrived in the US during the six-month-long infamous Mariel boatlift of 1980, the exodus that became best known for the unwanted element it brought – criminals and mentally ill people that Castro conveniently shipped out of the country. In reality, most *Marielitos* were like my friend: honest and hardworking people, eager to build a new life in the land of opportunity.

Back then, in the park with *El Grupo*, as we called ourselves, we did not dwell on politics, or whether we wished to stay or leave the country. That was for the grownups to worry about. We jumped rope to an infinite number of incantations, while our parents whispered and strategized. Sometimes, when the weather was bad, we played in our large covered balcony. It was not uncommon for ten or more kids to end up in our house, which caused Ota considerable distress.

"Zeida, why do you allow all those *chiquillos* (kids) to come into the house? It is not right! You don't know if they come from respectable families!"

But Mima paid no attention. She was always willing to accommodate us and occasionally we got her to join us in our games or act as referee.

The academic environment continued to challenge us in unexpected ways. Mima received a note that *mi hermana* would not pass 6th grade. *Mi hermana* had always excelled at school. Throughout her young life, she had been accustomed to being every teacher's model student and *Abuela* Mami's pride, so the note came as a big surprise.

Mima went to the school to find out what was the problem. The teacher informed her that it had nothing to do with *mi hermana's* academic work. All 6th grade students were required to attend after-school indoctrination classes sponsored by the G2 - the Cuban intelligence police - and *mi hermana* had missed one of the sessions.

"But Zeida María was sick that day and she had to stay home. I sent a note to the school," Mima said.

"I'm sorry, but those are the rules."

"Well, can she make up the session now?"

"No, we are not able to do that. There are no makeup sessions."

Mi hermana was frantic, Mima was very upset, and *Abuela* Mami was outraged. How could a student fail, other than for sound educational reasons? Then *Abuela* Mami thought of Consuelo, our former tutor.

"You know, Zeida, Consuelo is now a teacher at that same school. Perhaps you should talk to her to see if she can intercede on Zeida María's behalf."

So Mima called Consuelo at home. Mima and *Abuela* Mami had long suspected that Consuelo supported the revolution, but she was also a reasonable woman and she was well acquainted with *mi hermana*'s academic abilities. She agreed to look into the matter.

Thanks to Consuelo, the administration became more conciliatory. They agreed to let *mi hermana* move to the next grade on the condition that she'd take a test to answer questions about the Cuban Revolution and Marxist-Leninist principles.

Mi hermana answered the questions satisfactorily and she moved on to the 7th grade.

Chapter Twenty-Two

The Papi Connection

WITH THE FLIGHTS *Havana-to-Miami cancelled, there were only two other ways to leave the country. One was Mexico and the other one was Spain. Via Spain it was very expensive, as we had to pay the tickets for a plane from Cuba to Spain and then from Spain to the US. Via Mexico it was less expensive, even though we could not afford it either. Anyway, I wrote to my brother asking him to claim us via Mexico, hoping that if it was possible I always could try to get dollars from good friends that were in the States.*

[Early in 1963] my brother claimed us and after several months he wrote to us:

"Be ready. I have been informed that your application is in the last steps."

To be ready meant to have all our papers in order. Birth certificates, marriage certificates, my divorce, my father's death, all had to be translated to English and legalized at the Swiss Embassy, which represented the US *in Havana. That meant about $200 that I didn't have, so, illegally, I sold my Encyclopedia and paid for it. The notice from the Mexican embassy never came.*

Everyone who was attempting to leave the country felt as we did: thrown into a pool of uncertainties without a lifejacket. Many started taking their chances at sea, but the ninety-mile journey proved to be more treacherous than if the Himalayas separated the US from Cuba. Boats were sometimes stopped at the outset by the authorities guarding the Cuban coastline. Those that made it out to sea often sank because they were in poor condition or overcrowded with hopeful passengers, or fell victim to stormy weather. Back in the 60s, those who cleared Cuban waters on small vessels, rafts, even inner tubes, were typically rescued by the US Coast Guard and brought to Miami. Today, they are sent back to Cuba unless they touch US soil before being captured.

My mother was not at the point of considering an escape in this fashion, but it was shortly after the Missile Crisis that we heard about Papi.

Mi hermana and I were at the pharmacy with Mima. She was hoping to find aspirin for her chronic headaches, and Sacarías, the pharmacist, leaned over the counter to speak with her. "Do you remember the lady with the two daughters that used to live close by?"

"Yes...," my mother responded.

"Well, some of my friends told me they saw the girls' father." He paused and then said with a peculiar intonation, "He was over their way."

"Really?"

"Yes, it's true."

I was clueless about what was going on, but *mi hermana* whispered in my ear, "They are talking about Papi. Sacarías just does not want other people to know."

I often relied on *mi hermana*'s astuteness. She whispered again in my ear, "Sacarías told Mima that Papi is in the US."

"How do you know?" I asked.

"Just by the way he is talking and how carefully Mima is listening."

Our father had not visited us for some time. Nobody, not even *Abuela* Mami, had heard from him. This was not in itself unusual. He lived in Havana. We were used to not hearing from him for long stretches of time. However, we were surprised at the news. Mima believed that Papi sympathized with the revolution. So why would he leave the country, and how?

Soon after our encounter with the pharmacist, *Abuela* Mami received confirmation from the underground that the rumors were true: Papi had left illegally and was now in the US. "Best news I've heard in a long time," she said. "People are expecting me to cry, but I'm jumping for joy."

Our father had been part of our lives off and on during our early childhood. When he lived in the upstairs apartment of *Abuela* Mami's house with his third wife and baby, *mi hermana* and I dropped in every Sunday after church during our weekly visit to *Abuela* Mami. Mima, of course, stayed downstairs. But in less than a year, he left Sylvia and Orlandito, and moved back to

Havana. It was a familiar cycle. As before, *Abuela* Mami looked after his abandoned wife and baby until they too moved away.

I'm not sure how Papi made money in Havana, but I suspect *Abuela* Mami helped him. Despite her disappointments and frustrations, her love for him knew no bounds. He came to Camagüey once or twice a year, and *Abuela* Mami's joy was evident every time she announced that he was coming. The news made *mi hermana* and me burst at the seams with anticipation. He owned a car - a novelty in our world - and we liked to be seen in it with him, riding around town. We wanted our friends to see that, like them, we also had a father.

He let us eat *churros* and cotton candy at the amusement park. With him, we dared to go on the Ferris wheel, and finally, the ultimate ride, *La Montaña Rusa*, The Russian Mountain – a rollercoaster that compares to the present-day rollercoaster as miniature golf to a full-blown 18-hole course. Still, it was a great adventure for us.

He also took us to see *Sonia La Patinadora* perform on a real stage. Sonia was a roller skater. She was a master of athletic grace and balance who did all kinds of twirls and jumps, and splits in the air. Her energetic and cheerful presence made every feat look easy and fun. She regularly performed in the park or on the streets unannounced, pulling off amazing feats with those dark-skinned, muscular legs springing out of her scanty shorts.

Everyone knew about Sonia. She was something of an illusion. In spite of her bright lipstick and the ribbons in her hair, Sonia was a man. There was no hint of manhood in her appearance, but it was a well-known fact, and this duality added to her charisma.

There came the day when she no longer surprised children at the park. She, like Papi, disappeared from our world. I often wonder what became of her, since her kind did not meet the revolution's seal of approval.

However, Papi did come back into our lives. Ironically, the near-suicidal escape – as we would later find out - of the man who once upon a time stole my mother's heart opened the one window that eventually allowed us to leave the country after our failed attempt through the port of Camarioca.

Chapter Twenty-Three

Rite of Passage

THE CUBAN EXILE COMMUNITY in Miami, in direct defiance of Castro's orders and in total disregard of international laws, continued to conduct raids against Cuban targets. In addition, they often flew over Cuba, dropping propaganda leaflets.

One day, *mi hermana* and I, upon hearing planes flying above us, climbed up the stairs to our rooftop.

"Here is a pamphlet! Here is a pamphlet!" *Mi hermana* said, and before I had a chance to look at it, she was running downstairs to show Mima.

The pamphlet had the image of the Virgin Mary and a prayer.

"What does it mean?" I asked. "Do you think the prayer contains a hidden message?" I wondered why something as innocent as a prayer would be dropped from a plane coming all the way from the US. I expected to read something more along the lines of "WE ARE COMING FOR YOU. DON'T GIVE UP. YOU WILL BE FREE!!!"

Visits to doctors and dentists had always been a dreaded affair for *mi hermana* and me. In our younger days, we spiraled into a panic attack upon the appearance of a needle, pliers, or any shiny instrument other than a stethoscope. I call it the power of two: normally, *mi hermana*, being the oldest, would go first, and I tuned into her well-being. As soon as I detected the slightest discomfort on her part, any signs of anxiety, I began to panic, and then it was too late. Our frenzy fed and bounced off of each other like a swarm of attacking bees.

It was true that Mima made it easy to run away from needles, throw a temper tantrum, or even stomp on someone's foot, because her attempts to control us were mixed with loving acceptance and resignation. Instead of threatening us with a beating, she pleaded and tried to reason with us.

In the end, her tactics worked and we succumbed to our fate. Trusting only her - with our breath still skipping - we let out the faint sob of defeat. The doctor, or the dentist, after regaining composure, carefully carried out their work, making sure Mima was their intermediary. Out of respect for my poor mother, who in their eyes deserved a trophy, we were never turned away.

I was glad to hear that our old dentist had left Cuba, and Mima would take me to see a new dentist. Anyone would be an improvement over the sadist Mima called "our" dentist, the one who had removed a few of my baby teeth. The one who bore my teeth marks in his hand.

Now I was older. I was determined to behave bravely. Perhaps with a new dentist, it would be possible. I did not suspect that our new dentist, trained by the revolution, would refuse to use anesthesia on cavity fillings.

I remember Mima sitting next to me, holding my hand as the dentist started to drill.

She begged for anesthesia when she saw me squirm under the pain, but he was resolute. Anesthesia was in short supply; it could not be wasted on fillings, even when the cavities were as deep as mine, he told her. Mima did the only thing she could do. She gripped my hand tightly and comforted me. "It will soon be over. Everything is going to be fine," she said, as the smell from the drilling pierced my nostrils.

She later told me how proud she was that I behaved so well, but I could tell she was upset. She suspected that the real reason anesthesia was not available to us was because we were *gusanas*. The dentist charged her a hefty sum of money after remarking that he knew who we were. He did not care that Mima no longer had a job. Clearly, we must have had something stashed away.

More than ever, Mima was determined to leave this land that she once had called home, where we were no longer welcome.

Meanwhile, I was afraid that perhaps the cookies I had eaten at *Abuela* Mami's house had caused my cavities.

One Sunday, not long before my cavities appeared, I had gone on one of my exploration missions in *Abuela* Mami's house. It was fun to look through her drawers and wardrobe, but it was even better to scout her kitchen. Much like Mima, *Abuela* Mami had no use for aesthetics. There were no pictures, flowers, figurines or any other decoration to soften her home's appearance. There were taxidermied animals – a large frog and a turtle she called Caribe among them. On top of her furnishings in the dining area she had massive pickle-jar-shaped containers that had been in her classroom back during her days of teaching Biology.

Through the murky solution inside the jars, I could see the remains of different types of creatures - creatures that had at one time roamed among the living. One was a large coiled snake. All but one jar seemed to hold complete organisms. The other held a piece of *Abuela* Mami herself. Mima told us that after *Abuela* Mami underwent surgery some time in her past, she had asked the physician for the clippings. Who knows what it was - an organ gone bad? A growth? I walked past the dining area into the pantry, averting my eyes from the jars in hopes of avoiding recurring nightmares.

I could usually find a bottle of soda, a fig, or a banana in the pantry. This time, I probed the darkest corners of her shelves and found a dusty but very pretty tin can. I had seen tins like this one in Mima's sewing area. Usually they were filled with buttons and pins and other things. I dusted it off, opened it, and to my surprise, it was full of cookies. All different types of cookies, nicely stacked inside ruffled white paper holders. They were similar if not identical to what I know today as Danish cookies. They were sooo pretty. Some looked like flowers with a red center. Others were topped with crystallized sugar. They all looked mouth-wateringly good, so I asked *Abuela* Mami if I could eat some of her cookies.

"What cookies?" she asked. I showed her. "Oh yes, I had forgotten about those. Go ahead and eat them," she said.

I told *mi hermana*, but at that moment she was busy with a game, so I decided to save her some for later.

I started to eat the cookies. Delicious! I savored the mixture of sugar and butter as I tried one of each kind, and then I had seconds from each group. I was going to have one more and leave the rest for *mi hermana*, but as I reached for that last cookie, I detected something moving near the bottom of the tin can. I shuffled the cookies around to get a closer look and there they were...little worms sneaking around.

I ran to show *Abuela* Mami. She looked, and said, "Oh, we'll need to throw these cookies away. What a pity." Then she studied the worms. "These are little inch worms. Look how they slide in and out, in and out."

I was secretly glad that I had not noticed the worms right away. The cookies had been such a treat, and it had been so long since I had eaten anything but beans that it was worth a few worms in my belly.

At least that's what I thought, until the cavities appeared. Then I was sure those creepy little worms had gnawed through my teeth and caused each one of them, particularly since *mi hermana* did not eat the cookies and her teeth had no cavities. What further scientific proof did I need?

Mi hermana had a different type of dental problem that also needed attention. Her upper front teeth were protruding from habitually biting her lower lip, so Mima took her to a woman orthodontist, a friend of a friend, and the orthodontist confirmed Mima's suspicions. Zeida María needed braces. The cost was high, but the orthodontist knew about my mother's situation, so she suggested that *mi hermana* only wear braces on her upper teeth since her lower teeth were not in bad shape and not quite so noticeable. She only charged Mima for the materials, and *mi hermana* got her badly needed braces.

I don't know how Mima was able to cover all of these expenses, but she managed to make ends meet. Almost every afternoon she had seven or eight students around the dining room table – all needing help with Algebra. Then, of course, there was the monthly stipend that the government was paying Ota for the properties they had confiscated. She did not know she would be forced to repay that money before leaving the country – not until the Camarioca fiasco in 1965.

The shortages in Cuba continued to mount. By 1964, the subjects of food, and how to obtain it, dominated every adult conversation and became an obsession in every household. Just as, years earlier, communism was a topic woven into every discussion, food was now the subject even at weddings and funerals.

One afternoon, turning a corner on her way to school, *mi hermana* accidentally bumped into a woman carrying three eggs wrapped in a newspaper. The eggs dropped and every single one broke. The woman looked at her eggs on the sidewalk, slumped down, covered her face, and began to cry. *Mi hermana* could not stop thinking about it for days.

I came home one day to find a wonderful surprise: *Tío* and *Tía* had sent us a care package from Miami – this was after Mima had sent them a list of the most important provisions we needed. The Cuban authorities often inspected packages from abroad before they reached their destination, and it was common for many items not to reach the intended recipient. Still, the arrival of a package from the US, even if it had been tampered with, created an excitement reminiscent of the arrival of a newborn baby. Everyone came to see and admire the goods.

In our package, *mi hermana* and I got our first commercially-made training bras. To cover our budding breasts, Mima had made bras using scraps of cotton material and reused elastics. They were as uncomfortable as they were ugly, often sagging and creating unwanted bulges under our clothes. In contrast, our new bras from the US were snow white, with elastic around the torso that allowed movement without displacement. The best part was that, in between the small cups, there was a delicate little flower. I proudly showed my girlfriends, who proceeded to take turns trying on my new bra and admiring the tiny flower, a sure sign of elegance. On a couple of occasions I even managed to lend it out in exchange for a chance to wear a pretty dress. The shuffling of goods had become a common transaction in our world.

Thanks to the care package, *mi hermana* and I also no longer had to wear the stale-white cotton bloomers Mima had made from reused fabric, with elastic that cut into our thighs and waist. *Tío* and *Tía* included a beautiful assortment of candy-colored jersey panties, each with a different English word denoting the day of the week, Sunday through Saturday.

The pristine garments we received and Mima's stories about the US made me picture what our lives would be like if we ever reached its shore. Not only would it be bright and clean, but also trusting. In the US, Mima said, the grocery stores had aisle after aisle of goods on the shelves for anyone to take and then pay for on their way out.

"What keeps people from stealing?" I'd ask.

"The honor system," she said. "It's the same with newspapers. They are often unattended. You take one and deposit the money in a container."

Imagine that: the honor system. How different from Cuba, where goods were always behind the counter to avoid rampant theft. Revolution or not, Cubans suffered from lack of respect for the establishment. Perhaps it was a desire to get away with as much as possible in a country where people were used to being taken advantage of. Perhaps it was a way to undermine authority in a place with a long history of political corruption.

Whatever the reason, I knew it would be different in the US. I fantasized about my life in that other world, a world overflowing with abundance, where everyone was honest and kind, and shared a common pride for the established order. Like a budding anthropologist, I extrapolated from facts and artifacts to the inherent characteristics of the North American people and their culture, and I came to the conclusion that I would fit in. Everything in our lives would be planned and orderly, our clothes would carry the never-before-worn scent of newness, and we would feel welcomed among the warm and friendly people. Our lives would be the antithesis of our Cuban existence.

As an added bonus, the care package also contained Lifesaver candies and, best of all, chewing gum - Chiclets, Juicy Fruit, and Double Mint. This was the epitome of luxury. It not only tasted heavenly, but it was so cool. It was like advertising to everyone that we had connections in the US.

The gum lasted a long time: we cut each piece in half, sometimes in fourths, and at bedtime, I often saved the chewed gum to chew it again the next day. I discarded it only when it was so bland that chewing on a rubber band was slightly more gratifying, or when Mima spotted a chewed piece and said, "Marina, you've got to get rid of this, it's disgusting."

Gum was convenient in other ways. Like prisoners who trade cigarettes for privileges, children in Cuba used gum to get favors. Someone always was willing to do something for a piece of gum: tell a juicy secret, lend a pretty dress, invite you to a party, do your homework – anything was possible.

Chapter Twenty-Four

Our Turn

I NEVER LOST MY FAITH, I trusted God to solve our problem. In my own country I was treated as an outsider by the government people. On the other hand, I was held in high esteem by those who did not agree with the government.

Three years had passed since *Tío* had claimed us through Mexico, but we were still waiting. The boat he sent to Camarioca in 1965 left without us, as related earlier. Because of it, *Tío* lost his savings, and we continued to be stranded in Cuba - this time without any money.

Another painful effect of the Camarioca fiasco was that I had to come to terms with the fact that Rondy had to stay in Cuba. While waiting for the telegram that never came, Mima found a new home for Rondy in the countryside. I'm pretty sure it was the farm he had originally come from. So, after six years of being a house-dog, Rondy went back to the farm. *Mi hermana* and I were instructed to go to a nearby bus stop with him, and a man would come to take him away. We did what we were told, handing his leash over to a complete stranger. Trembling, Rondy turned back to look at us; the sadness in his eyes revealed his awareness that we were abandoning him.

We never saw him again.

After the port of Camarioca closed, I asked Mima if we could get Rondy back.

"No," she said, "we still need to be ready to leave the country at a moment's notice and we cannot take him with us. Besides, I hear that he likes his new home."

I rarely questioned my mother's sincerity, but I did not believe her this time. Rondy was so used to living in our house; how would he survive on a farm? I was convinced that he had already become dog meat, but I did not pursue the matter further. Even I could tell that Mima could not handle any more issues at this time, so I never mentioned Rondy again.

Soon after Camarioca, the US and Cuba reached an agreement to reinstate chartered flights from Cuba to Miami five days a week, each carrying 200 Cubans. Named the "Freedom Flights," they were intended to reunite families, thereby addressing the tragedy of the 14,000 Operation Pedro Pan children who had been in the US for more than three years without their parents. Accordingly, priority was given to parents with minor children in the US, or vice versa. However, Cuba did not allow young men of military age to leave the country. So, parents who had children in the US but also had sons of military age in Cuba, or daughters married to men of military age, had a difficult decision to make. Also, professionals such as medical doctors and people with skills deemed essential to the revolution were prohibited from leaving, which thwarted the reunification of some families.

In our case, we were not hindered by any of these restrictions.

My ex-husband was in the USA and my girls were still minors, so I asked his mother for his address and telephone number and I called him. As he had left the country illegally, if they found out, we would not be allowed to leave, but thank heavens his name was so common in Spanish that the possibility was remote. I also asked my brother to claim us. In February 1966, while I and my daughters were at the funeral of the mother of the girls' piano teacher, I got a call from my mother. A telegram had just arrived and we were allowed to leave the country. I couldn't think it was for real and at the same time, I was afraid that at some moment something would happen that would interrupt our plans.

This time I didn't have problems in the bank. They came to check our belongings and no problems arose. About the few clothes we were allowed to bring with us they only objected to the sleeping clothes. But still I would have to go through another hazard. A short time before, I had sent our 4 passports to the Ministerio de Emigración to be [renewed] as they were almost [expired] and I still didn't have them back. I went to the office in Camagüey and they told me they did not have them yet. They still were in Havana. Next day we should be in Havana and then we could get them there.

So, we left Camagüey. The last hours, an amazing number of friends came to say goodbye. When the bus left, many were crying and among them my youngest girl.

Valentine's Day was our last full day in Camagüey. It was, thus far, the most emotional day in my young life. Many of Mima's former students and friends came to bid us farewell. Mima and her friend Hortensia said goodbye, not knowing when they would see each other again. Hortensia had been Mima's friend since the days when they were both students at Havana University. She had been Mima's faithful companion during her summers in New York City, and her only close friend to remain in Cuba. Hortensia stayed because her mother refused to leave the family farm behind.

Also, on our last day in Camagüey, we went to say goodbye to Paula Collado and her family, the former owners of the apartment building where Cuca had lived. Paula showed us a box of Uncle Ben's rice, which she was saving for a special celebration she'd hold the day Castro fell. "Any day now," she said. When it was time to go, Paula's aunt, a very delicate and fragile older woman who rarely rose from her rocking chair, struggled to her feet and walked us to the door, leaning heavily on her cane. It was a solemn moment that filled me with intense sadness; I hugged her hunched little body tightly, and as I let go, she lost her balance and fell backward, cane and all. Everyone gasped.

"Ayyy Marina…" I heard Mima say. In that instant, the notion of getting a fresh start in a place where people were not familiar with my past seemed quite attractive.

Everyone hovered around the old woman, helping her back to her rocking chair "I'm fine... I'm fine..." she said. "It was nothing, really..."

While the commotion still lingered, we left Paula's house. We never saw them again.

During our last year in Cuba, *El Grupo*, our group of *gusano* friends, had grown to include boys as well as girls. These boys were just entering military age, and therefore were not permitted to leave the country. Their future was uncertain, as Castro's government prepared to help Algeria and other African nations in the fight against imperialism and exploitation.

In the early evenings, *El Grupo* would get together, put on some records, and dance, dance, dance. We danced to salsa music and Cha Cha, but we also danced rock 'n roll, and we even managed to find a few songs by the Beatles. All of this was done discreetly, since entertainment without a revolutionary message was frowned upon by a regime that stressed discipline, and endorsed militant chants for its youth:

Estudio, Trabajo, Fusil! (Study, Work, Rifle!)

At the age of twelve, I was the youngest one in *El Grupo*. I was always in *mi hermana*'s shadow. She was fourteen, had a boyfriend, and was very popular. I tried to model my behavior after hers, but that was not enough to welcome me into the inner circle of *El Grupo*.

Nevertheless, dancing was my favorite activity and I was pretty good at it. I was never short of a partner, except during the slow numbers when the boys preferred to dance with someone older and less tomboyish than I.

That last evening in Camagüey, *mi hermana* and I went to a friend's house for our last dance. Janet had one of the best collections of music from the 50s. She had boxes and boxes of albums that her older brothers had accumulated over the years, and her house lay in back of the family store, where it was impossible for anyone in the street to hear the festivities. We danced to the tunes of Elvis. We did the Twist, and we grooved to Paul Anka. At the end of the evening, all of us, sweaty and tired, joined in a final Conga line around the entire house. I kept thinking that there could not possibly be anything more fun than this moment in time.

Early the next morning we got on the bus headed to Havana. *Abuela* Mami and many of our friends who had said goodbye the night before came to bid us farewell.

"Don't forget to write!"

"We'll miss you. I wish we were going with you!"

"Don't forget to send us gum!"

I began to cry. I would miss my friends, my hometown, but mostly, I would miss *Abuela* Mami, who, upon seeing my tears, told me, "Don't cry! This is the best thing that has ever happened to you! You are a very lucky girl." But the more she talked, the more I cried. Her image then and there, in a bright, colorful dress - strikingly at odds with her stern face - would forever be imprinted in my memory.

I took one last look at Camagüey. Paint was peeling from buildings and houses, windows were broken, and dilapidated balconies lined the streets. The bus was in equally bad shape.

The seats were rusty, the fumes were strong, the engine was loud, and the entire bus vibrated. Only a miracle would get it to Havana without incident.

And it did.

Of the possessions we left behind, the only one that I would miss – besides Rondy - was the piano. It had been six years since *Abuela* Mami and Ota enrolled *mi hermana* and me in musical training. On many occasions we had protested and begged to stop, but nobody listened. After the torturous hours of practice, the endless frustrations and feelings of inadequacy, I had actually become attached to this instrument.

Mi hermana and I played popular duets with our friends - chopsticks, Heart & Soul and Blue Moon. Popular Cuban tunes like Almendra reverberated through our home. *Mi hermana*, always the dutiful student, had mastered a number of pieces by classical composers like Bach. I preferred Mozart, but my favorite composer was Ernesto Lecuona who, in many ways, was the Cuban counterpart of Gershwin.

La Malagueña, his most masterful achievement, was entrenched in the classical Spanish tradition, but *La Comparsa*, my favorite, was deeply rooted in the Afro-Cuban style. It is a short piano rendition of a Carnival Procession. It starts softly, imitating the distant beat of the bongos as the carnival approaches, then grows progressively louder, the rhythms more complex. It climaxes in a musical feast for the senses, and then recedes as lightly as it arrived.

The music of Lecuona was forgotten in revolutionary Cuba. He had moved to the US soon after Castro seized power, and he vowed not to play the piano publicly until Cuba regained her freedom. He died in exile in 1963 at the age of 68.

When we arrived in Havana, Paco, the famous surgeon who was Mima's uncle and Ota's brother, picked us up at the bus station in his 1959 Chevrolet. After the long bus ride, his air-conditioned car provided us with a heavenly ride through Havana. It looked so different from either Cienfuegos or Camagüey. We drove through wide open avenues, marveled at the tall buildings and at the sounds of the waves crashing against the wall of the Malecón.

Just to ride in a car was a treat for us - a distinct sign of luxury, particularly if it was from the US, rather than from the Soviet Union.

Mima left some of her possessions with Paco: family photos, letters and announcements with sentimental value, and a few pieces of jewelry. These would find their way to Mamatita's house in Cienfuegos, the place where everyone in the family stored their valuables before leaving the country.

While *mi hermana* and I explored the posh neighborhood of Miramar where Paco lived, Mima tied up the loose ends concerning our departure:

> *Early next day I went to the Ministerio looking for the passports. They told me they had been sent to Camagüey, but that I could leave without them. That night we had a nice farewell dinner at my uncle's and then we went to a big house that had belonged to a very rich family that left the country.*

El Laguito, The Little Lake – that was the nickname of the mansion close to the former Havana Biltmore Yacht and Country Club, where everyone leaving the country was required to congregate the evening before their flight. When we arrived, the main hall and courtyard of the mansion were already full of people - men, women and children, sitting on chairs and benches, on the steps and on the floor. All 200 passengers scheduled to depart that night were arriving.

Mima wrote her name on a list and began to settle us down for the long night ahead. She found a place for Ota to sit, and stacked our *gusano* bag – the only luggage allowed - against the wall. The bags were tubes approximately three feet long, similar to laundry bags. The dimensions were strictly enforced, so we, like most *gusanos*, had brought our fabric to an experienced *gusano*-bag-maker. The contents of the bag were also strictly enforced: one change of clothes per person, one pair of shoes, and one sweater.

Mima was told that after all passengers were processed, we would be taken by bus to Varadero, an hour's ride from Havana, to catch a flight scheduled to depart at 7:00 the following morning.

Mi hermana and I asked if we could go out into the courtyard, and Mima said, "You can go, but the two of you need to stay together and don't go too far away. If our name gets called, you need to come back here IMMEDIATELY."

I wondered what made her so agitated. At the time I did not have a full appreciation of everything that could go wrong. There was the issue of the missing passports. Also, the authorities might inquire about how our father had left the country. In addition, I did not know it at the time, but Mima was carrying jewelry. It was her insurance policy - what if she needed money in the US? Hidden inside her vagina was a prophylactic sheath with the sapphire bracelet given to Ota by Mamatita on her wedding day, the sapphire pendant given to Mima by Ota on her wedding day, and the diamond earrings that Oto had given to Ota when they married.

On top of everything else, she had to take care of Ota.

It was written on my mother's face - the feeling that this opportunity, likely to be the last one, and so close within our reach, could easily slip from our grasp at any moment.

In the courtyard *mi hermana* and I struck up a conversation with a family from Santiago - a boy and a girl, and their parents. The father asked us, "How many persons in your group?"

"Four. The two of us, our mother and our grandmother."

"No father?"

"He is already in the US. Our parents are divorced."

"So your mother is on her own?"

"Yes."

He and his wife looked at each other. He said, "Your mother is a very brave woman to attempt a trip like this on her own."

"I could not do it. I'd be too afraid," his wife added.

I thought this was a peculiar reaction. I had seen my mother under considerable stress. I had seen her frustrated and upset. I had seen her anxious and agitated, even desperate, but I had never seen her afraid. Was fear a state only married women could allow themselves to feel? I wondered.

I went to see how Mima and Ota were doing and I was relieved to see that my mother had found a place to sit. I told her about the conversation with the family in the courtyard. Mima pulled me close, and said, "Whatever you do, please don't talk about your father with anyone. No details to anyone, please. If people ask, just say you don't know."

It seemed to me that Mima was overreacting, but I promised I would not mention Papi again, and I would tell *mi hermana* to do the same. I got Ota a cup of water and went back to the courtyard to get away from them. Mima was irritable and Ota was pale.

Ota's diabetes had taken hold of her. She was sweating and hallucinating. "*Mamá*, please don't get sick," Mima tried to soothe her. "This will soon be over and you'll get to see your son the moment we arrive in Miami. Just close your eyes and try to get some rest."

Around 2:00 am, *mi hermana's* name was called, since she was the one in our group who was claimed by our father. Mima jumped to her feet and screamed, so that the entire place could hear it, "Zeida María, Marina, please come, we are being called!"

Embarrassed, we rushed to Mima's side to put an end to her loudness. We picked up our *gusano* bag, and marched to the place of call.

We sat down in another waiting area and Mima filled out a form - names and relation of all persons traveling, dates of inoculations and the reason for wanting to leave the country.

"Who is claiming your family?" she was asked.

"The girls' father."

"Do you have anything of value on you?"

"No," she lied.

"How about the girls and your mother, do they have anything of value on them?"

"No."

She was not asked to produce the passports.

A physician reviewed our inoculation records. Mima asked him, "Can you take a look at my mother? She is diabetic and not feeling well."

He went to Ota, looked into her eyes, felt her pulse, and listened to her heart. "I think she is very nervous," he said. "Let me give her something to calm her down."

He gave her pills to take and said, "If her condition deteriorates any further, she will need hospitalization and she will not be able to travel with you."

Mima prayed that this would not be the case. She was not going to leave Ota behind.

Perhaps the episode with Ota disrupted an already disorganized procedure. The doctor did not perform the routine body search for illegal possessions.

At the crack of dawn the buses were loaded with luggage and passengers, and in the very early morning hours we arrived at the Varadero airport. The air was cool and a layer of fog covered the ground. I had taken a short nap in the bus and now, walking to the airport terminal, I hoped to hear one last time the sound of the waves and breathe in the fresh ocean air. But it was not meant to be. I thought it ironic that my last glance of Cuba was from the place of my most cherished childhood memories, a place we had not seen for a few years.

At the airport everyone was served a North American style breakfast with ham and eggs. Already the surroundings seemed foreign. The food was definitely different, but the most remarkable change was that there WAS food and it was free. I was almost too tired to eat, but I could smell the ham, and I could not pass it up. The eggs tasted quite different than what I was used to and they had a strange consistency.

"I think these are powdered eggs. They are very common in the US because they are easy to prepare and can be kept for a long time, not like fresh eggs," Mima explained. Amazing, I thought. What will they invent next?

There were other signs of changes to come. The plane's crew talked to one another in English. Tall men wore nicely-tailored uniforms, and women, also in uniform, wore fashionable leather shoes and tight-fitting translucent nylons. Makeup covered their faces, and their smiles were framed by beautiful shades of lipstick. It was a glimpse of our new world – perhaps I would some day look like that. I was hopeful.

They gave us a good breakfast and then they called family by family. I was scared to death that there was still time for them to find out about my ex-husband's illegal departure or to bring up some objection for not having the passports. I saw that each one who was called presented their passports and they stamped something in them. When we were called I said I didn't have the passports but they didn't object. Then I saw what was stamped in them: Nulo (Null). We were not Cuban citizens anymore. After the plane started and I thought we must be far enough as not to be ordered to come back I started relaxing. This time it was for sure!

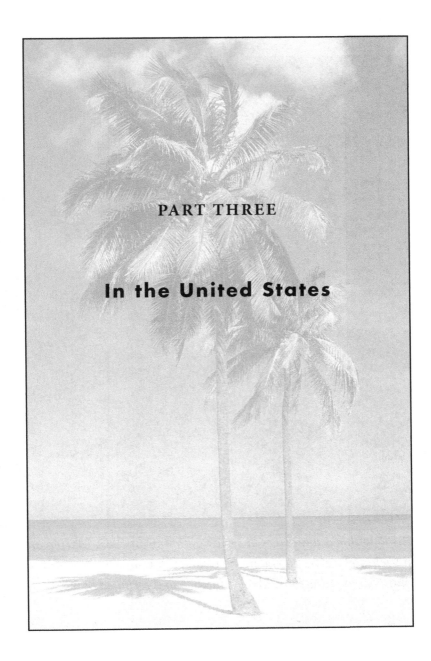

PART THREE

In the United States

Zeida with her daughters in Hinckley, Maine in 1967. Marina on the left and Zeida María on the right, both wearing the corduroy outfits Zeida made in Cuba for the trip to the United States.

Chapter Twenty-Five

Finally in Miami

WHEN WE ARRIVED IN Miami, Mima was forty-five years old, Ota was seventy, and *mi hermana* and I were fourteen and twelve, respectively. Our North Americanization process began immediately. The agent from the Department of Immigration advised my mother to abandon the Villa name in favor of her estranged husband's surname. And so it was that my mother, for the first time in her life, was known by Papi's name. She became Zeida Rodriguez in order to have the same family name as her two daughters.

Refugees coming into Miami on the Freedom Flights were encouraged to settle in other areas of the country, since Miami was overflowing with Cubans.

"New Jersey or Louisiana would be your best options," the immigration agent said to Mima. "You will be given room and board, and a stipend to cover basic needs until you can find a job. In Miami you will not receive any further assistance."

Mima thought about how much colder New Jersey would be. The agent said, "The Salvation Army will provide you with all the necessary winter wear. You will not have any problems settling there."

"Okay, then we'll go to New Jersey. But is it possible for us to stay with our family in Miami for a few days? We have not seen them in a long, long time."

"Of course. We can book your flights in a week, if you like."

After paperwork, medical examinations and shots, we finally saw *Tío* among a multitude of people waiting for their loved ones. "Ota! Ota! There is *Tío*. See him through the window?" Ota's demeanor changed instantly. Once we exited the building, he was there, hugging Ota, and then Mima.

"*Ay hijo*, what an ordeal! I have not slept in days!" Ota told him.

"Mamá, we are going to take care of you. Don't worry, from now on everything will be fine."

"Just seeing you makes me feel better."

Mima asked her brother for a cigarette. Between puffs she informed *Tío* of our plans. "I was told that my chances for finding a job are better in New Jersey."

Tío looked disappointed. "Zeida, you should have said that you had family in Miami and were staying here. We Cubans take care of each other."

"Well, it's too late now," Mima said. "Besides, this way we won't be a burden to anyone, and I think they are right. The prospects of me getting a teaching position here are very slim."

Tío said, "It does not really matter. We'll all be back in Cuba within nine months anyway."

But Mima did not see it that way. We were in the US for good.

When we arrived at the small efficiency apartment where *Tío, Tía* and Bichi lived, *Tía* was putting in the oven pie-shaped bread with a tomato sauce and cheese topping. It was called pizza, a very popular dish in the US, we were told. *Mi hermana* and I were not in the habit of refusing food, so we didn't, but we both agreed that the aroma was more enticing than the pizza itself. It was too foreign a combination for our palates to appreciate. As we ate and talked, a continuous flow of their Cuban friends dropped in to meet us and to congratulate us on our arrival. There were many personal stories, and a lot of advice, particularly when we said we were headed to New Jersey. Most of them had hardly ventured outside of *Calle Ocho* and Little Havana, but that did not stop them from painting a picture. "You better take a good shower before you leave. People up north can't bathe in the winter. It is too cold!"

"No, that's impossible"

"Yes, it is true. I know because the friend of a relative of my brother's wife said so. That's why Americans keep to themselves. It is not that they like privacy; they just can't stand to smell each other." Everyone laughed.

I felt that we had entered a happier and prettier version of Cuba. Everyone spoke Spanish. The streets were spacious and straight. There were grassy areas, palm trees and flowers. It was as though the city had been spun with a magic wand - a far cry from Camagüey, which could have been carved out of concrete with a crooked chisel. In Miami, every car looked new and every structure modern.

The people laughed and talked freely. When someone poked fun at President Lyndon Johnson, I gasped. "You should not say that. Someone might hear you!"

"Here you can say whatever you like. This is a free country!" I was told.

Later that evening, we went to the small house shared by Concha, Marta, Pepito, Yolanda, and their three children – where Panchita and Felix's daughter Mercy had also lived until she got married.

Everyone was there. And everyone brought clothes to donate to the help-the-new-refugees cause. We received a lot of slacks. In Cuba, women – except Cuca - wore dresses or skirts. Now it seemed pants were the norm and I could not wait to join in.

Mercy was now 23 years old and married to a very nice young Spaniard. She begged for news about her parents, and Mima told her how Felix had helped us when she needed money to pay Ota's debt to the government. It was her father who loaned Mima the $1,500 she so desperately needed at the time of her ill-fated attempt to leave through the port of Camarioca. Mima told Mercy that once she got a job, she would pay her the money. That's what Felix had requested.

Mercy cried. She talked about reuniting with them, about them meeting her husband - but how? Felix was 73, and Panchita was 65. Coming to Miami to start a new life was not in the cards for them. Felix was incapable of leaving the tobacco farm that had been in his family for generations. He still considered it his no matter what the government said.

After the family reunion at Concha's, Bichi, now 20, took *mi hermana* and me in his car on a scenic tour of Miami Beach. It was breathtaking. The glimmering lights, the high-speed highways, even the traffic was fascinating. I wanted to become part of this world that I had only seen in movies long ago. I pictured myself on a boat with Tony Curtis, like Marilyn Monroe in "Some Like it Hot." I could be Doris Day, chased by the likes of Rock Hudson. I would wear outfits inspired by Lauren Bacall and have a flat in a high-rise building. The future held boundless possibilities. Bichi pointed at the boats on a pier and said, "Someday I'll take you out on the water in my own boat and we'll go water skiing." I believed him. When we passed a beautifully groomed golf course, he said, with disdain, "This is how rich old people spend their time. They hit a little ball and then get chauffeured around so that they can hit it again. They don't even break a sweat. Where is the sport in that?"

None of our relatives had enough room in their homes to accommodate the four of us, so during our week in Miami, Ota stayed with Concha, Mima and *mi hermana* stayed with Mercy, and I stayed at *Tío* and *Tía's* efficiency apartment. There, I learned to take showers carefully. First, the bathroom curtain rod at *Tío's* was bent beyond repair. In the absence of a gym, Bichi had used it for chin-ups. While I found this fascinating, a symbol of male power and strength alien to me, it made it difficult to keep the shower curtain in place, and the water from splashing all over the bathroom floor.

Then there was the water temperature. The hot water was scalding; I had to use both the cold and hot water faucets to find a delicate balance. And without warning, the temperature might shift to either arctic or cooking levels depending on what else was happening in the building. In Camagüey I never paid attention to the hot and cold faucets. Each produced lukewarm water.

When *Tío* asked me if I wanted to go to the grocery store with him, of course I said yes. I wanted to experience the honor system that Mima had talked about.

The store was immense. I could not fathom how there could be so much food in one place. We walked into the produce section, with bins of bananas, oranges, and apples. I loved bananas and oranges, but apples were a rare delicacy for me. The few I had eaten in my lifetime had been juicy, sweet, and crispy in a way that no other fruit could duplicate. My mouth watered just looking at them, and more so as their exquisite bouquet reached my nose. When *Tío* said I could pick one, I was immediately overwhelmed by the different varieties. So I picked the biggest, reddest, shiniest apple in the bin, under a sign that even I could read: delicious clearly meant *deliciosa*.

We walked through aisles with shelves stacked with boxes and cans and bottles. When we got to the rice, I saw a familiar name: Uncle Ben's. But there were others, and the rice image on each box was as appealing as the next. Rice had never looked so good on my plate - that was certain.

"What's the difference?" I asked *Tío*.

"Ah. Not much. Different companies sell rice. We look for the cheapest."

Tío did not pick Uncle Ben's.

Everyone was loading their carts with goods from the shelves, and nobody was keeping tabs.

"But what happens if you don't have enough money for everything in the cart?" I asked.

"Then we take some out."

It seemed simple.

In the cookies aisle, *Tío* told me to get whatever cookies I wanted, but I did not know what to pick, and I was just happy with my apple. I had not yet discovered the wonders of an Oreo. Instead, I asked *Tío* if he could buy me gum, and he did.

In the car, I took the much anticipated bite of my beautiful red apple. I was expecting a heavenly flavor like no other. Unfortunately, reality rarely lives up to the imagination. The apple was not as sweet, or as juicy, as I expected.

When *Tío* was at work, I helped *Tía* around the house and accompanied her on her errands – another chance for me to explore this new world. We walked into a store, and *Tía* warned me, "When you see *Norte Americanos*, try not to talk because they don't like us and they don't like to hear Spanish spoken in their country. They are afraid that the Cubans are taking over."

I remained quiet and watched closely those who might not like us. I knew what it was like to be treated as a second-class citizen by *Fidelistas*, but I was confused by the rejection from people I admired and wanted to emulate. Obviously, they did not know us Cubans, and that's why they were upset. *Tía* pointed to a sign outside one store that read, "We speak English." I laughed, but she said, "*Norte Americanos* don't see any humor in that. They are disturbed and insulted by the fact that people can conduct business in their country without speaking one word of English."

While our wardrobe kept growing, we still needed shoes, so Mercy and her husband took us to a shoe store and offered to treat *mi hermana* and me to a new pair. I had never seen so many beautiful shoes in my life. It was better than any assortment of chocolates. How could I select only one pair? As I sat there, having my foot measured, I heard Mima say to Mercy, "I'd like to get the girls some sensible shoes that they can use for school."

Mi hermana and I looked at each other. There was no way I was leaving the store without the black patent leather shoes I saw in the window. So the shoe salesman brought pair after pair of nice sensible shoes for us to try, and after walking a few steps, I'd say, Mima, they hurt my little toe, my big toe, my heel, my arch. Finally, I said: "Let me try these other ones…oh yes, these are perfect! I can walk miles with these patent leather shoes."

I walked out of the store wearing patent leather shoes with my newly acquired red gingham pants from the donation stash. I felt gorgeous.

Notwithstanding the cultural friction, Miami was the epicenter of Cubanity, and everyone in our family thought Mima was crazy to leave. But we already knew Cubans who had ventured north. Cuca and Baldo were in upstate New York, where Cuca taught Spanish at a college. *Tío* had notified her of our arrival and, through her, the entire Camagüeyan diaspora was informed. Also, *Tío* contacted some of his old friends from Preston who lived in New Jersey. We would not be alone.

Chapter Twenty-Six

A Taste of New Jersey

We boarded a plane to Washington DC with a connecting flight to Newark, New Jersey. When we landed in Washington, snow was falling, a sight I associated with Russian movies. I found it fascinating until we went outside. Despite the Salvation Army green wool coat, winter hat, and gloves, the cold penetrated my core. The warmth of my body took flight with each visible breath as we descended the plane steps and walked to the airport terminal. This new world was both beautiful and frightening.

Swarms of people robotically rushed through corridors, climbed escalators, and passed through doors that automatically opened. Everyone was on a mission. Double doors trapped the warm air inside and protected people from the menace of nature, exactly what I would have expected had we landed on Mars.

Spanish was no longer spoken. I was an alien, and my only connection to this strange land was Mima who, in broken

English, asked for directions and then navigated the course. I kept close to her, as did *mi hermana* and Ota.

In Newark we were taken to a boarding facility that had seen better days as a hotel. The sign still read "Hotel Carlton." It was reserved for Cuban refugees and funded by the Volunteer Relief Agencies, to which Catholic Charities was a major contributor. We were provided with a room and three meals a day until we could find an apartment within our rental allowance.

Homesickness set in. I feared I would never see the sun shine again – something I had taken for granted all of my life. The dry heat inside made my nose bleed, and the cold outside made my lips crack. The snow was dirty. The people in the street were impersonal, always in a hurry and, like the weather, seemed harsh and cold. No one made eye contact or offered a friendly smile. *Mi hermana* and I, trapped in a stuffy room with a noisy heater, spent our days watching TV without understanding a word. Every day I asked Mima if we could please return to Miami.

But Mima could not have been more appreciative. "What a wonderful country," she said. "We come here without a cent, and we are given food and a roof over our heads, no questions asked. There is no other country in the world that would do this!" After going hungry, or spending months eating only beans, she could not understand how anyone could complain about the taste of the cafeteria-style food, which was void of *sofrito* – the familiar sautéed onions and garlic that's the essence of every Cuban dish.

She was determined to make it work. Every day, she bundled up and went to look for an apartment in areas *Tío's* friends had recommended. Within a few weeks she found a small place in East Orange, right outside of Newark. It was furnished with the basics, thanks to charitable donations.

Mima went to a nearby parochial school to see if they would accept *mi hermana* and me for the remainder of the school year. The nuns took us in and provided us with uniforms free of charge. Mima could not stop talking about our fortunate circumstances and the generosity of the people. Her unrelenting good spirits were beginning to wear on *mi hermana* and me, and we responded by rolling our eyes, and praying for her to stop.

The nuns at the school were kind to us. They placed us in regular classrooms with our age group, but attempted to teach us English by bringing us books meant for young children learning to read – I remember Spot the dog. It was so boring that I spent most of the time daydreaming. We learned a few words, but we still could not understand what people were saying. However, we did not need to know English to do math, so when the class worked on math problems, *mi hermana* and I were the stars. The nuns could not believe our proficiency, and we could not believe we were so much more advanced than the other students. At home, with Mima and a dictionary, we began to decipher math word problems, thereby learning English at the same time. We had learned problem-solving from Mima at an early age, and for the first time in my life, I saw its true value: it provided a much-needed boost to a deflated ego.

Luckily, two other students at the school were from Ecuador, and the four of us became friends. They were sisters and had been in the US for a year. They could translate for us. We found a niche, and thus were not totally isolated.

Mima looked for a dentist to fill my usual set of cavities. Through the Volunteer Relief Agency, she found someone willing to treat me. I was a perfect patient. With anesthesia, the experience was no longer horrifying.

The dentist examined *mi hermana*'s teeth, which had started to protrude because her retainer had to remain in Cuba.

"Excellent orthodontist work! Was the orthodontist trained in the US?" the dentist asked.

"No, I believe she studied in Cuba," Mima said, proudly.

"A woman orthodontist? Really? She did a very nice job!"

It came as an unexpected cultural shock that, in the US, professional women were rare. We were much more accustomed to dealing with them in the *machismo* society that we had left behind. A society that accepted, respected, and even admired highly qualified women, although such status came at a dear price: as Ota had warned when Mima went to Havana University, they seldom married.

One day, Cuca and Baldo came from upstate New York to visit us. Even *mi hermana* and I were happy to see Cuca. We tried our best to show that we had outgrown our childish pranks, and Cuca quickly embraced our more mature behavior. As soon as she arrived Mima and she began to argue, just like old times.

"Cuca, you have to stop sending me money. For now, I'm able to manage with the help I'm receiving."

"*Coño*, Zeida, I'm only doing it because I can," she said, as she took out her checkbook.

"Please put it away. You have already done enough," Mima said. "If I need money, you'll be the first to know."

"I would not offer it unless I had it, so stop being *majadera* (foolish)."

Mima stood firm. "I know, Cuca, that if there is anyone in this world that I can count on, it's you."

They were not in a position to give money away, and Mima knew it. Cuca was the only wage earner. Baldo was much older, and he was not adjusting well to life in the US. He never mastered the English language and he was prone to depression. His outlet became art; he drew beautiful Cuban scenes from memory and, since most of them were black and white, they blended perfectly with Cuca's black and white decór.

Life could not have been easy for them in Plattsburgh, New York, an isolated town just south of Montreal - a place too cold for the flipflops, shorts, and halter top that she loved to wear. But Cuca did not talk about hardships in front of us.

Soon after Cuca and Baldo's visit, Rosita Martínez, another teacher from the *Instituto* who was teaching at a University in New Paltz, came with her sister to visit us. They brought Mima winter clothes and some nice outfits so she could make a good impression during job interviews. Mima had already started looking for work. She had told the employment agency that she was willing to take a teaching job anywhere in the country.

Rosita and her sister gave Mima job-hunting tips from their own experience. Rosita's sister was, in particular, full of advice.

"Zeida, don't gain weight. You can't let yourself go. The most important thing when looking for a job is to look good. This is not Camagüey. Here, qualifications are not as important as how you look. You cannot look old, or worn out, and you need to watch your weight. In this country, looking nice is not only for the young people. If you don't wear makeup, shave your legs, and wear nice clothes, forget it," she said. "You are lucky because your hair is not gray. My hair was almost white and I could not get a job. I went from interview to interview, and I got rejected everywhere. Then I dyed my hair, and I got the first job I interviewed for."

Rosita's sister introduced us to Spanglish when she asked for an "espoonita" to stir her coffee.

"'Excuse me' are the two most useful words in the entire English language," she told Mima. "In any type of situation, when you get too close to someone, or brush against them in an elevator or a bus, then you are expected to say 'Excuse me.' If you want someone to get out of your way, then say 'Excuse me.' If someone looks annoyed, even if you don't know why, just say 'Excuse me.' You can do almost anything you want, if you just follow it with 'Excuse me.'"

To the delight of *mi hermana* and me, soon after we arrived in New Jersey, Papi, who was teaching Spanish in New York City, came to visit us. He continued to come on a weekly basis. He bought us a TV, bought us clothes and ice cream, and bought Mima a badly needed grocery cart so she would not have to walk almost three blocks carrying our groceries in her arms. On a couple of occasions he took Mima, *mi hermana* and me sightseeing in New York City, and once, we went to see the Rockettes at Radio City Music Hall. It was like old times, when Papi took us on outings around Camagüey - except that now, Mima was included.

We asked him how he had managed to leave Cuba. He told us he had rented a rowboat and rowed out to sea, determined to cover the ninety-mile distance from Cuba to the Florida

Keys. In order to avoid suspicion, he wore a swimming suit and brought no drinking water. He had planned to row for one hour and rest for a half hour, but the current kept pushing him back toward Cuba, requiring him to row constantly. After three days at sea, he was picked up, unconscious, by the US Coast Guard and taken to Miami, where he recovered from dehydration, exhaustion and third-degree burns.

In East Orange, Ota got sick to the point where she needed medical attention. Mima and Ota took a bus to the nearest hospital. But the hospital turned them away: they would not accept a patient unable to pay for treatment. Mima was directed to another facility, but after a long bus ride, Ota was refused there as well. They again took a bus, to a third place that was, they were told, certain to provide medical care for the indigent. By this time, Ota was barely able to walk. At the third hospital, the staff took down Ota's information; since there was no insurance or government program to pay for the health services, they again rejected her. Mima pleaded, "Please, we've been going from place to place looking for charitable medical care. We are from Cuba and we have no money."

"I'm sorry, but you have to apply for government assistance before we can take her in."

"But she is very sick and I don't think she can wait. Is there any way she can get help?"

An administrator approached Mima and asked, "Are you Cuban refugees?"

"Yes, we are." He turned to the staff and said, "By law we have to take her, even if they cannot pay."

So Ota was examined. Her blood sugar level was out of control and she needed to be hospitalized right away. Mima returned to the apartment to recount the ordeal, and the next day the three of us went on the long bus ride to visit Ota at the hospital.

We were directed to a large hall with two rows of bed, all of them occupied by very sick people. Most of the patients were elderly or demented. The atmosphere reminded me of the rows of beggars lined up outside the church in Camagüey. Everyone seemed desperate for help and, since I could not help them, I avoided eye contact. We found Ota on a bed three quarters of the way down. Her usual controlling demeanor was gone, replaced by an expression of anguish and defeat. When she saw us, she said, "Ay Zeida, go away, please go away…"

"*Mamá*, what's wrong? What's the problem?"

"I'm in terrible pain…I need to urinate…but I can't…they put something inside me that does not let me pee."

Mima rushed to get help while *mi hermana* and I remained by her side. For the first time in my life, I felt sorry for Ota.

Ota's catheter was obstructed so she could not relieve herself. The room was full, and sparsely staffed, and Ota could not speak English; she did not know how to call for help.

At last, the attendant came and drew the curtain around Ota's bed. *Mi hermana* and I stood outside the curtain; we heard Ota groan, then the sound of urine like water blasting from a fully opened faucet, in concert with an explosion of gas. *Mi hermana* and I, embarrassed, glanced at each other and then at those around us. But everyone was too consumed by their own miseries to mind the loudness of Ota's farts.

After this, we visited Ota every day to make sure that she was all right.

Throughout that summer in New Jersey, Mima searched for a job. She had several interviews, some as far away as Alabama, but no offers, and the school year was fast approaching. If she could not get a teaching job by September, she would look for other alternatives. Perhaps she could work in a factory, like some of the other Cubans we knew.

In August, she was invited to interview at a college in San Luis Obispo in California. *Mi hermana* and I were delighted with the prospect of moving to California - a place that on TV seemed even better than Miami. We kept our fingers crossed. As soon as Mima returned, she had another interview lined up at a boarding preparatory school in Hinckley, Maine.

None of us had heard of such a state, so we first had to verify its existence on the map. Main with a silent 'e' at the end, we were told. There it was, close to Canada - far, far away, in the too-cold-to-wear-flipflops zone of the North Country.

Mima was in Maine when a telegram arrived from San Luis Obispo offering her the job. *Mi hermana* and I were ecstatic. We were on our way to join the surfers on the sunny beaches of California and we could not wait to tell our mother.

When she returned, she looked as if the weight of the world had been lifted from her shoulders. She had been offered the job in Maine teaching math, and had accepted it. The job included room and board for all four of us, a modest salary, and free schooling for *mi hermana* and me. What else could she ask for?

"But Mima, a telegram arrived from San Luis Obispo. You got the offer! We should go to California instead!"

"Oh no, I've already given my word to the people in Maine. I cannot go back on my word," she said.

"Ay Mima, please, please, please. They'll find someone else. The people in California need you as much as the people in Maine. PLEEEEAAAASE!"

"No, we are moving to Maine. You'll see that it is not as bad as you think. The people are very nice. There is even another Cuban family that teaches at the school. I met them. They like it there and I know that they will help us."

Without further delay, we took our oversized green wool Salvation Army coats - coats that might as well have had REFUGEE stamped across the back - and off to Maine we went.

Chapter Twenty-Seven

Maine and Beyond

THE HINCKLEY SCHOOL LAY alongside the Kennebec River, a river still used at that time by loggers to carry logs to the sawmills downstream. We had landed in Paul Bunyon country. The pine trees, the dense woods and the wooden houses, even the squirrels, were foreign to us.

We got to Maine just in time to enjoy the magnificent New England fall foliage - nature's palette at work. At every turn there was an explosion of vivid colors accentuated by the sunlight. "Is it always like this? ...What causes it?" we wanted to know. "This is even more beautiful than the paintings I've seen," Mima said. "I thought the artists exaggerated, but in fact, they didn't do it justice."

The crisp country air in Maine was refreshing - a far cry from the thick smog that covered Newark. Everyone we met was nice, but distant. They tried to make us feel welcome. The faculty and staff donated clothes and other items for us to use. We were showered with wintry wear. Someone gave Mima a used sewing machine, and she started to alter the clothes to fit us. After a snow storm, neighbors came to help with their shovels, and if it was a very cold day, they would ask if we wanted a ride to the school building. When we needed a ride to town, someone was always willing to help us.

Mima saved enough money to buy a used car and taught herself how to drive it. She had her share of fender-benders. As with the bike in Varadero, people learned to stay out of her way when she was behind the wheel.

The first day she got the car, she asked me if I wanted to go for a ride just around the circle in the school road. The problem was that she had to drive in between two cars. She was inching her way through, at turtle speed, when she hit one. Then she backed up and hit the other. She stopped right there, sweat coming down her forehead, went to the house on the circle, and told them she had hit both of their cars, that she would pay for damages. The young teacher was understanding, and agreed to drive her car back to our driveway.

The most difficult driving challenge was, of course, the ice and snow. *Mi hermana* was with her when she slid right onto an oncoming car. Fortunately, nobody got hurt; 20 miles an hour was the speed limit on the old school roads. She got out of the car and started apologizing in an agitated state, while *mi hermana* kept telling her, "Mima, *en inglés por favor!*"

One day Mima took all of us to Pittsfield to visit another Cuban family. It was her first long distance trip, one hour away. On the way back, in the dark, she followed the Fernández car – another Cuban family who had recently found work at the Hinckley school. After a while on the interstate, Luis Fernández stopped his car on the side of the road. He climbed out and walked over to our car. "Zeida, I think we took the highway in the wrong direction. I don't think we should be seeing headlights coming toward us."

He was right.

We were lucky. It was after 9:00 PM, and in Maine that meant most everyone was home for the night. We made a U turn and took the next exit.

Teachers at the school were eager to give *mi hermana* and me the extra help we needed. The English teacher gave us different books than the ones he gave to the rest of the class. I remember Bambi. *Mi hermana*, the dutiful student, meticulously studied English every night. She read the assigned homework with dictionary in hand, and asked Mima for help with grammar. I was less academically inclined. I skimmed Bambi, and got the gist of the book. I learned English mostly by going outside the dorm, where students were allowed to smoke, and listening to conversations as we puffed on cigarettes. Math continued to be our niche throughout high school. I stayed at the top of my class, although *mi hermana* was far more gifted in the subject.

Our immersion in the English-speaking environment yielded results: a year after arriving in the US, *mi hermana* and I could speak English fairly well, and people acted surprised when they found out that we had only been in the US for a year.

Soon after we arrived in Maine, Mima started a photo album. The first page had two pictures from Cuba. I don't know how we had these, since no one was allowed to bring pictures out of the country - they were routinely confiscated by luggage inspectors. I suspect Mima packed them, thinking that if they were taken, so be it. One was a passport-like photo of *Abuela Mami*, with her typically stern face. The other was a picture of Rondy, with his beagle-mutt face and his stubby tail. It had been taken by a photographer upon Rondy's first-year anniversary with us. He was probably one and a half years old. He was posed on a small rug, barely lying down, his ears astutely perked and his skinny legs ready to spring into action.

On cold winter days in Maine, I took the photo album to my room. I missed them so much; the pictures warmed my heart, and made me yearn for the life we left behind.

For despite all the extra help we received from the faculty and staff at the Hinckley school, these were very difficult times for *mi hermana* and me through our teenage years. We were not used to the courteous but reserved ways of the natives. We were lonely. We had very limited social lives. We did not fit in with the other students, and we could not fit in no matter how hard we tried. Our clothes, our accents, our dark curly hair at a time when the fashion called for girls with straight hair to straighten it even more – all of this gave us a foreign air that was difficult to ignore.

To top off my misery, I suffered a horrendous attack of acne.

We were completely out of our element. We missed the tropical air, but mostly, we missed *El Grupo* - the fun and laughter, the music and the dancing, the gossip and the flirting that were part of our past. We missed simple, carefree social interaction.

Mi hermana and I began to sink into depression while Mima was busy taking care of our basic needs. I don't think Mima ever knew the depth of our despair, the severity of our shared condition. Perhaps she thought ours was a common teenage angst. Perhaps the many years of worrying about food, clothes, and keeping a roof over our heads had numbed her. Or perhaps she was suffering her own depression.

Mi hermana and I didn't talk to anyone; we slept through the weekend with curtains shut and the light off. During my waking hours I watched TV incessantly. I was so jealous of all those people on TV on the beautiful California beaches. Would I ever be able to wear a swimming suit again?

In time, we found avenues to deal with our misery. Mima got us a puppy. *Mi hermana* concentrated on academics. I found comfort in the old piano at the cottage where we lived. Out of tune, with missing and muted keys, it was still playable. Inside the piano bench there were old music sheets that had turned yellow, but I could decipher the notes. I taught myself some of the music – Beethoven's Moonlight Sonata, Chopin's Minute Waltz, Schubert's Ave Maria.

The music teacher at the school, Mr. Bender, helped and encouraged me. One day, he brought me a piece of music that he thought might interest me. It was *La Malagueña* by Ernesto Lecuona. He had ordered it after he heard me play *La Comparsa*. "If you love Lecuona, then you should learn to play his best work," he said. "It will not be easy, but I will help you." And he did. Under his guidance I practiced and practiced *La Malagueña* until I mastered it. In this way, I gradually started to let go of the past without forgetting my roots.

One day we learned that *Abuela* Mami was sick. She did not tell us in Cuba because she did not want to burden us with her problems. When we got settled in Maine, we occasionally placed a call to her in Cuba. It often took an entire afternoon to make the connection, as the operator queued our call, and we waited for a response back indicating that the call was going through. The last time we talked with her, we could barely understand what she was saying. She had cancer of the throat; with great effort she asked Mima to tell Papi. She wanted to hear from him before she died, but by then, we and Papi had already drifted apart.

Papi came to visit us regularly when we first moved to Maine. He had developed a new interest in us, and Mima and Papi were considering getting back together. While *mi hermana* loved the idea, I was not happy. All my life I had had only one parent and I wanted to keep it that way. Luckily for me, Mima reconsidered. After an argument concerning *mi hermana* and me, Mima asked Papi never to return, and we never saw him again.

But Mima had his address. He had moved to Albany, where he was teaching Spanish at the local campus of the State University of New York. She notified him about *Abuela* Mami's health, and how much she wanted to hear from him. Not long after, she wrote one last letter to him to tell him that *Abuela* Mami had died.

As we grew older, *mi hermana* and I realized that *Abuela* Mami had been the first feminist in our lives. "If there are going to be social consequences for a woman who has a child out of wedlock, there should also be social consequences for the man who fathered the child. It is only fair," we heard her say - not a common view in a society that encouraged men to carry out their fantasies. She led by example. She was not a woman to shy away from her principles. It was she who had filled the void left by her son, for the care and wellbeing of his children.

Throughout high school *mi hermana* and I became very close. I continued to devote my time to music and other artistic endeavors, and *mi hermana* focused on math. She was always first in her class, and started calculus before her senior year. In contrast, I received first prize for weaving.

We eventually adjusted, but it really wasn't until after high school that *mi hermana* and I formed the social connections that helped us find our place.

Ota was too old to learn English, so in Maine, she led a very isolated existence. She could only socialize when we got together with the other three Cuban families – two in Hinckley and one in Pittsfield - who probably constituted the entire Cuban-American population of Maine.

Mima always marveled at how Ota never complained about the loneliness, about missing her family in Miami, about the cold and dark winters. Once she had made up her mind to follow Mima to the US, Ota gave up the airs of a General, and became a General's aide to Mima. Still, old habits die hard: I can remember her sitting in a chair, carefully watching Mima sew, and giving her instructions on how to do it right, in the same manner that she used to direct every cook she ever had in Cuba. Mostly, Mima ignored her, but every once in a while, she would say, "Mamá, have you ever sewn anything in your life?"

"No."

"Then let me do it my way, Okay?"

"Ay Zeida, I'm only trying to help."

I graduated from high school when I was about to turn 17. I told Mima that I did not want to go to college. I wanted to become a dancer. This was against Mima's steadfast belief in education, particularly for women. I'm certain *Abuela* Mami was also turning in her grave to hear such heresy out of me. But Mima knew she could not make me do something I didn't want to do, so she agreed to pay for me to stay at the YWCA in Bangor and take dancing lessons. I was young, and she hoped that in a year I would be ready for college.

In Bangor, I started going out with a young man I had met through *mi hermana*. He was a student at the University of Maine in Orono, where she was also attending school. In a year's time, instead of going to college, I was walking down the aisle. Mima, as always, kept an open mind and hoped for the best.

Soon after I married, Mima lost her job. The Hinckley school had been hit with a legal suit that led to a change in its charter, and to high litigation costs, and Mima was one of the casualties. She moved to Massachusetts and started teaching at New Bedford High School. My husband and I moved to the Boston area where he found work after graduating from college.

One day while visiting Mima in New Bedford, I told her that I wished I had gone to college.

"Ay Marina," she said, "you and Ed can move in with me, and I'll help you pay for college."

So my husband and I moved to the basement of her tiny house in New Bedford, where we lived rent-free for my first two years of college. We then moved closer to where my husband was working, and I finished my undergraduate studies at Boston University. Mima was so proud of me.

Mima lived in New Bedford until she retired in 1983. My husband and I settled in New Hampshire, and *mi hermana* served in the Peace Corps, and later settled in Miami.

As the years passed, Ota became more docile and dependent on Mima, but every once in a while the General re-emerged.

All her life Ota had enjoyed reading the newspaper. Mima had started a subscription for her to *El Diario Las Américas,* the Miami-based Spanish newspaper, back in Maine; the paper and the Lawrence Welk show were Ota's main sources of entertainment. She read the newspaper cover to cover, often out loud, interjecting her own commentaries.

Then, one day, when they were living in New Bedford, Ota asked Mima to stop the subscription. Her eyesight was deteriorating, she said, and she could no longer read it.

Mima reluctantly did as requested, but it was hard on Ota. In fact, it was impossible. The newspaper had become Ota's lifeline. So every day, Ota picked up the English-language New Bedford newspaper that Mima received, and read it as thoroughly as she had read *El Diario.* It did not matter that she could not understand the language; she made up her own interpretation of events.

Mima asked her again and again if she wanted to resume the subscription to *El Diario*, but Ota always responded, "No, no, no, no, no, Zeida. I cannot read. It hurts my eyes."

She continued to pore over the English newspaper. She read it out loud, with fervor, pausing after every word, and pronouncing the English as if it were Spanish. She added authoritative, if imaginative, commentaries and regaled Mima with her version of world events.

Once, Ota told Mima about a tribe in Alaska that had made the newspaper headline: the US government had to send many men to deal with tremendous problems created by "Los Peepaeleenae de Alaska."

Mima was intrigued. She had never heard of the Peepaeleenae tribe. She read the headline. *"Mamá,"* she said, "you mean the Alaskan pipeline. There is no tribe. Peepaeleenae is pronounced pipeline!"

"Oooooh, that's what it is…Why would anyone want to build a pipeline in Alaska? It's crazy to go to such a cold place!!!"

Ota died in 1980, on the day that my first husband and I drove to New Bedford to tell her and Mima that I was pregnant. She had a heart attack before we arrived, so she never heard the news about the baby.

About six months after Ota died, Mima visited me one Saturday in my home in New Hampshire. This was a weekly tradition she had started with Ota and then continued by herself. I lived about three hours away from New Bedford, so she normally arrived around noontime and left after an early dinner. On this particular Saturday, she helped me shop for a crib. It was late when we finished and she was tired, so she decided to sleep over and go back to New Bedford on Sunday morning.

Mima always arranged her Sundays around the Mass schedule. By staying over, she would miss her usual 9:30AM Mass, but she would get to New Bedford for the 11:00AM service.

She drove off in the morning as planned, but her car started making an awful noise as she drove through Boston. She waited at the side of the road until a mechanic from a nearby garage came to help her.

He said that the car muffler had come loose, and offered to tow the car to his shop so he could fix it on Monday. "But I need to get home to New Bedford today," Mima said.

The mechanic tied the old muffler back in place, and told Mima, "You need to drive slowly and tomorrow you need to get it fixed."

Mima inched her way to New Bedford. It was almost 4:00 PM when she got there, time for the last Mass, so she went directly to the church.

As she sat in the pew, wondering how to get the muffler fixed on Monday and still get to school to teach her classes, the service opened with the announcement, "This Mass is offered in memory of Isabel González."

Mima was dumbfounded. She had walked into the first of three Masses she had requested in Ota's name after her death. A Mass she had every intention of attending, but had forgotten due to the six month wait.

Had Ota caused the day's misfortunes?

The last words Mima had said to Ota before she died were, "Mamá, if there is an afterlife, send me a sign if you can." This, in Mima's eyes, was her mother's sign, but perhaps not the last command from the General.

Ota's biggest regret was not being able to pass on to those she loved any of her properties. Modest as these were, for Ota, it was her legacy and, ultimately, how she thought she would be remembered. Instead, we remember her as the strong-willed woman who would stop at nothing to help her family, who treated men as kings, and most of all, who got the last word even after death.

Perhaps she still has plans for her beloved properties in Cuba.

Epilogue

Thank You, Mima

OUR LIVES TODAY ARE very different from the days when we struggled to find our way in the United States of America. *Mi hermana* and I have enjoyed successful careers in the computer field, and we both are fortunate to have loving family and friends.

Bichi gained financial success beyond his or anyone else's expectation. Within a year after we arrived in Miami, he started pre-med at Rutgers University in New Jersey on a full scholarship. He then attended Harvard Medical School. He has been the president of *La Liga Contra el Cancer* – League Against Cancer- in Miami for many years. He became a very successful doctor and a wealthy man, able to provide for his parents and his family in grand style. Most importantly, he kept his word: he took us waterskiing in his boat as he once said he would. He also became addicted to playing golf, joining those rich old men he so vehemently criticized.

For the most part, Mamatita's descendants were able to establish themselves and re-build their lives. But there were casualties. Panchita and Felix's daughter, Mercy, tried to maintain some hope of one day reuniting with her parents in Cuba. As time passed, she fell prey to deeper and deeper bouts of depression. In 1978 Concha called Panchita in Cuba to tell her that her daughter had died of heart failure. She was 37. Concha never revealed the overdose of sleeping pills to them; even so, Panchita and Felix lived the rest of their lives with irreparable guilt and sorrow, suspecting that Mercy had ended her own life.

And there was Ota's brother Paco, the famous surgeon who lived in Havana. The exile – as some Cubans still call it – was most difficult for those who came at an advanced age. Paco was 70 when he immigrated in 1973 with his son and his family, after his wife died. He had exercised considerable clout in the medical community in Havana, and had been given the honor of *Hijo Ilustre* – Illustrious Son - in Cienfuegos, his home town. He died in Miami two years after his arrival, suffering from alcoholism and depression.

Mima lived with me after she retired from teaching, so I was her principal caregiver during the last years of her life. She died in 2009. Alzheimer's brings unimaginable pain and sorrow, but while she had some grasp of reality, she knew she was loved. Bichi welcomed her to his magnificent home during the winter months. *Mi hermana* showered her with gifts, visits and phone calls from Miami. She patiently worked with Mima on simple math problems, and read poetry to her. And while she was still somewhat lucid, Mima and Cuca had a few adventures together – like the time Cuca drove her from Miami to New Orleans because Mima said that she had never seen the Mississippi.

Today, Bichi, *mi hermana* and I remain close, although we lead very different lives. At least once a year, we all come together as a family. To the amusement of our spouses and children, none of whom are native Cubans, we launch into noisy, passionate political arguments in typical Cuban style. If political debate was a competitive sport, Cubans could hold their own, or perhaps they would be disqualified for not following the rules. We exaggerate, liberally use gross generalities and shout and interrupt each other as if the safety of our planet depended on getting the final word. Bichi is always on the conservative side, while *mi hermana* and I uphold the liberal camp. Ultimately, having solved nothing, we make room for more wine and the tasty Argentinean Churrasco that Bichi expertly cooks on his barbecue grill. We celebrate our family bond, a bond reinforced by our common past, by the many obstacles we've faced together, and by the knowledge that, through it all, we could count on each other. It is a bond that goes far deeper than any ideological differences among us.

On one of these occasions we were debating how the Cuban-North American population might react when Castro's regime in Cuba ends. Will Cuban descendants in the US want to move back to Cuba, and perhaps claim the properties that belonged to their families nearly fifty years ago? Will they try to influence, or even control, the new Cuban government? Will they buy vacation homes and invest in the new Cuban economy? What will happen? In the midst of our heated discussion, *mi hermana* shouted:

"Thank you, Fidel! Thank you, thank you, thank you!!"

She was referring to the fact that, thanks to Castro, we had come to this country. All three of us believe that our lives in our adopted country are much better than they would have ever been in a Democratic Cuba. We can lament the hardships we faced, the challenges and the depression of our early years in this country, but we would not trade our life here for a life elsewhere. Cuba is our past, the nectar for our nostalgia, but the US is our home. It is the place that took us in when we were desperate. It is the place that gave us the opportunity to provide a future for ourselves and our children.

While none of this would have happened without Fidel, our parents made it a reality. Behind every single immigrant family, regardless of ethnicity, there is a story about the struggles that precipitated the leap of faith to abandon what they knew – no matter how bad it was – and embrace the unknown. Each is set against the backdrop of world events, and, as unique as each story is, they share a common thread: courage, determination and hope. And in most cases, at the heart of their decision was the desire to provide a better life for their loved ones.

I heard my mother's story many times over the years, and then I heard it again during the disastrous interview for the immigrant documentary, when Judy asked, "Zeida, tell me why you left Cuba."

My mother said, "Well, mostly I just wanted my children to grow up in a free country."

My mother could not remember anything else, but this sentiment, this wish, and the hope that drove her to do what she did, went with her to her grave.

It is in awe of her accomplishments that I celebrate every immigrant. In my mind, my mother's generation is the Cuban counterpart of "The Greatest Generation." Since for me she exemplifies the fortitude, the spirit, the love and the hope that is the backbone of every immigrant's story, I'd like to end this book by saying, "Thank you, Mima."

Zeida in 2006 during her final years.

Acknowledgments

WRITING THIS BOOK has been a labor of love inspired by my mother's life, her indomitable strength in the face of so many challenges, her relentless love, and her steadfast protection of my sister and me. I have been fortunate in ways that I cannot fully explain, to learn from such a wise woman and to be cared for by such a loving mother. Every day of my life I'm thankful to have come into this world as her daughter.

One of the most endearing gifts from this project was getting to know Sue O'Neill. She says she is my editor, but in fact, she is my mentor and my teacher. She is also a dear friend.

Sue, a talented writer and editor, lived in the same town as I did, and met me for coffee. She educated me about the politics of agents and publishing – in her words, "This is not a good time to become a writer." Then she volunteered to read the first twenty pages of my work and quickly sent me her feedback. Her invaluable comments ended with these words: I think you have more work to do.

At that moment I knew I had stumbled on the person that could help me get my book into shape.

I have also been fortunate to be surrounded by family and friends who believed in me, supported me, and encouraged this project through every step of the way, even through its infancy, when its merits were doubtful and obscure at best. The list is long, but I want to acknowledge each for their unique contribution that made this project possible.

I thank my husband Jim Kerry for not laughing when I told him that I was going to write a book. Through years of work on this project he never once discouraged me, and during the year that I was unemployed, he never hinted that I should spend more time looking for *real* work. On the contrary, while his engineering nature is often at odds with such topics as history, politics, and social issues, he reviewed my work, found humor in my narratives, and demonstrated a genuine interest in getting to know Marinita better. I'm also extremely grateful for his unquestioning support of my roll as my mother's primary caregiver. By understanding what this meant to me, he made it easier for me to look after my mother day-in and day-out.

As I wrote this book, my daughter Alicia Wagner was constantly on my mind. I wanted her to appreciate the woman who had taken care of her while I was busy at work. There was so much more for her to know about the grandmother who dedicated her golden years to enriching her life. Alicia's pride in her Cuban heritage and her encouragement for my project forced me to work harder, to do my best, and to remind myself that my work was important.

I thank my stepson Jonathan Kerry, who pulled his mind out of cyberspace to read some of the chapters in this book and provided me with constructive criticism. He found it interesting to read about people he actually knew. This is a bigger compliment than you might imagine.

I want to thank those who provided me with information that helped to make this work multifaceted and insightful. For many whose stories are woven into the fabric of this book, going back in time and talking about what transpired so long ago caused emotional distress, sadness, and pain. In most cases they shared their experiences with me because they trusted me to handle their past in a thoughtful and sensitive manner. I hope I did not disappoint any one of them. Many thanks to:

Mi hermana, Zeida Heavener, who helped me remember people and events that were blurry in my mind. She provided me with many facts and a somewhat different perspective.

Bichi, Luis Villa, whose memories of his parents and their lives before and after the revolution broadened my scope and helped me capture the tragedy of the Cuban experience.

Paquito Patiño and his wife Isabel Patiño, who shared their poignant story about Paquito's imprisonment. Their willingness to reveal so much of themselves tempts me to write another book just to tell their story.

Marta Johnson, who provided me with information about Mima's life, especially the weeks Mima spent in Havana with her and her parents while waiting to give birth to me.

Ramón Patiño, for checking my facts, and making me feel I had written something worthwhile. For telling me stories about growing up in Cienfuegos with my mother and my uncle.

Yolanda Patiño, for giving me insight into Pepito's life as a devoted husband, father, and brother, and an avid rancher. Thanks to their children, Graciela Céspedes and Rodolfo Patiño, for fact-checking and for describing how it felt to separate from their parents at a tender age.

Paquitín Monteavaro, for talking with me about his father's life and medical practice. Thanks for your determination to get Rafaelito and Ana María out of Cuba, and your dedication to help those in need.

Rafael Bustamante, for sharing details about Mamatita's house, and Cienfuegos.

Montserrat Peralta, better known as Cuca, who spent hours talking to me about life in Camagüey, my parent's romance, and the events that led to their separation and divorce. I thank her for her detailed account of the violence she witnessed at the *Instituto*. When I asked her if she remembered that day, she said, "*Coño*, Marina, of course I remember. There are some things in life that one can never forget."

Margarita Ortega, for being a loving friend to my mother, for relating the effect of the revolution on the schools, the events that led to her family's decision to leave Cuba, and for providing insight into my paternal grandmother's life.

Rosita Cabrera, another of my mother's friends and colleagues, for describing the events that took place when my mother defended Cuca and Baldo in front of the government officials. For her knowledge of the social and cultural life in Camagüey.

Federico Samperio Ortiz, for explaining the reasons that prompted Mima's father to leave Spain in search of a better life in Cuba.

Many friends and relatives read and re-read my early drafts. Their confidence in me kept me focused. It was their voices I heard when I was in need of encouragement. I would like to thank:

Nancy Tullo, who read draft after draft, and provided positive feedback and suggestions; she also convinced members of her book club to read my book as though it was a book club's selection.

Gail Page, who edited and re-edited some of my earliest drafts without ever complaining about the continuous changes I sent her way before she had time to complete her review.

Virginia Maxwell, who from the distant state of Hawaii, sent comments that enhanced the structure and clarity of my work.

Vinod Johnson, who also read an early draft and provided me with a comprehensive set of comments on each chapter. After going through it once, he offered to do it again – a true sign of friendship.

Poet Michael Casey, for helping me structure and organize my work. It was his idea to move what became chapter one from its original place in the chronological narration of events.

Katie Casey, for providing a young person's perspective, for telling me to describe my mother's laugh, and for giving me a wealth of constructive feedback.

Becky Rowlands, for reading my work and telling me, "I ache to hear your mother's voice." This prompted me to include Mima's notes verbatim.

Cheryl Aronson, for fixing many stylistic errors, for allowing my story to make her cry, and for letting me know that she was "honored" to read my book.

My wonderful niece, Lourdes Machin, for providing me with valuable feedback. In retrospect, it is clear that only an act of love could make anyone finish reading my earliest attempts.

April Dawley, for her questions, keen interest, and positive feedback.

Joanna Yeh, for her objective assessment, sensitivity and interest.

Members of Nancy's book club, Regina Sarkozy, Marylou Linnemann, Nancy Fahey, and Caroline Shea, for taking my work seriously and assuring me that there was an interest in the subject of the Cuban experience and the immigrant struggle.

I would also like to thank those who showed an interest in reading my work while still in its infancy: Gloria and Geoff Wager, Kathleen Casey, Nan Sheldon, and Beth Ferrentino.

In this world of high-tech, I would be remiss if I did not also thank my computer for allowing me to write and re-write each one of my drafts. For letting me re-structure sentences on the spot, correct a tense, and re-word an analogy or metaphor. More than ever, my admiration goes out to the many writers who have turned out masterpieces without such help.

Notes

Part One: The Revolution

<u>Chapter One – Camagüey, Cuba: September 1965</u>

- Opening the port of Camarioca: García, María Cristina, *Havana USA*, 1996, Chapter 1, Exiles, Not Immigrants, 37-38.

<u>Chapter Two – Her Early Years</u>

- Machado Closes the University of Havana: Thomas, Hugh, *Cuba or The Pursuit of Freedom* (1971), Updated Edition, Chapter L, Machado: II, 591.

- University of Havana re-opens: Suchlicki, Jaime, *Breve Historia de Cuba*, Chapter X, El Fracaso del Reformismo, 120.

Chapter Four – Castro Takes Cuba: *El Paredón*

- Excerpts from Castro's speech were taken from the Castro Speech Database, a collection of translated speeches and interviews available from the University of Texas Latin American Network Information Center (LANIC). The database can be accessed from the following website:

  http://lanic.utexas.edu/la/cb/cuba/castro.html

  Castro's first speech to the nation from Havana:

  Castro speech delivered in ciudad libertad: 01/09/1959

Chapter Six – The Revolution's Early Impact

- Agrarian Reform: Thomas, Hugh, *Cuba or The Pursuit of Freedom* (1971), Updated Edition, Chapter XCIX, Agrarian Reform: Politics and Crisis, 1215-1216.

- INRA: Thomas, Hugh, *Cuba or The Pursuit of Freedom* (1971), Updated Edition, Chapter CIV, Cuba Socialista: I, 1322-1323.

- Cuba requests weapons from Soviet Union: Thomas, Hugh, *Cuba or The Pursuit of Freedom* (1971), Updated Edition, Chapter CI, A Sword is Drawn, 1270.-1271.

- CIA operation to invade Cuba and nationalization of US assets: Thomas, Hugh, *Cuba or The Pursuit of Freedom* (1971), Updated Edition, Chapter CII, The End of Capitalist Cuba, 1297.

Chapter Eight – Chaos and Repression

- Castro predicts US-led invasion: Thomas, Hugh, *Cuba or The Pursuit of Freedom* (1971), Updated Edition, Chapter CII, The End of Capitalist Cuba, 1298.

- Number of political prisoners: Thomas, Hugh, *Cuba or The Pursuit of Freedom* (1971), Updated Edition, Chapter CV, Cuba Socialista: II, 1351.

- Number of Cuban exiles: Thomas, Hugh, *Cuba or The Pursuit of Freedom* (1971), Updated Edition, Chapter CV, Cuba Socialista: II, 1354.
  García, María Cristina, *Havana USA*, 1996, Chapter 1, Exiles, Not Immigrants, 19.

- Cuban resistance against Castro: García, María Cristina, *Havana USA*, 1996, Chapter 4, The Evolution of Cuban Exile Politics, 122-126.
  Thomas, Hugh, *Cuba or The Pursuit of Freedom* (1971), Updated Edition, Chapter CV, Cuba Socialista: II, 1348-1349.

Chapter Nine – The Bay Of Pigs Invasion: April 1961

- CIA briefing to the Kennedy administration before the attack, and the administration's position on US support, and expectations from Cuban resistance to join in the attack: Wyden, Peter, *Bay of Pigs: The Untold Story* (1979), Chapter 4, At the Watershed, 160-161, 139. Thomas, Hugh, *Cuba or The Pursuit of Freedom* (1971), Updated Edition, Chapter CIII, The U.S. Prepares for Battle, 1306-1311.

- The plan and timetable of the invasion: Wyden, Peter, *Bay of Pigs: The Untold Story* (1979), Chapter 4, At the Watershed, 163.

- United Nations special emergency session to discuss aggression against Cuba: Wyden, Peter, *Bay of Pigs: The Untold Story* (1979), Chapter 5, The Attack Begins, 185-190.

- CIA ensuring Cuban invaders-in-training of US support: Wyden, Peter, *Bay of Pigs: The Untold Story* (1979), Chapter 5, The Attack Begins, 190-193.

- Damage inflicted on Cuban air force planes: Wyden, Peter, *Bay of Pigs: The Untold Story* (1979), Chapter 5, The Attack Begins, 193.

- US infiltrators in Cuba not informed of the attack: Wyden, Peter, *Bay of Pigs: The Untold Story* (1979), Chapter 6, Invasion, 245-248.

- Mass arrest of Cubans to curb an internal uprising: Thomas, Hugh, *Cuba or The Pursuit of Freedom* (1971), Updated Edition, Chapter CVI, Battle of Cochinos Bay, 1356, 1365.

- Suitability of the Bay of Pigs region for the invasion: Wyden, Peter, *Bay of Pigs: The Untold Story* (1979), Chapter 3, Reappraisal and Momentum, 104-107.
  Thomas, Hugh, *Cuba or The Pursuit of Freedom* (1971), Updated Edition, Chapter CVI, Battle of Cochinos Bay, 1362-1363.

- Dealing with the captured invaders: Wyden, Peter, *Bay of Pigs: The Untold Story* (1979), Chapter 7, Aftermath, 302-303.
  Thomas, Hugh, *Cuba or The Pursuit of Freedom* (1971), Updated Edition, Chapter CVI, Battle of Cochinos Bay, 1370-1371.

- Excerpts from Castro's speech were taken from the Castro Speech Database, a collection of translated speeches and interviews available from the University of Texas Latin American Network Information Center

(LANIC). The database can be accessed from the following website:

http://lanic.utexas.edu/la/cb/cuba/castro.html

Castro's speech celebrating International Worker's Day, after the Bay of Pigs invasion:

May Day Celebration: 05/02/1961

Chapter Ten – Paquito Goes to Prison

- Land Ownership in Pre-Castro era: Thomas, Hugh, *Cuba or The Pursuit of Freedom* (1971), Updated Edition, Appendix XII, The State of Agriculture in 1959, 1562-1563, Chapter XCIV, Sugar, 1146-1148.

- *Sierra del Escambray* as possible refuge to the Bay of Pigs invaders: Wyden, Peter, *Bay of Pigs: The Untold Story* (1979), Chapter 7, Aftermath, 309. Thomas, Hugh, *Cuba or The Pursuit of Freedom* (1971), Updated Edition, Chapter CIII, The U.S. Prepares for Battle, 1309.

- Operation Pedro Pan: Didion, Joan, *Miami* (1987), Chapter 11, 122-125.

Chapter Eleven – Aftermath of a Failed Invasion

- The Catholic church and Castro: Thomas, Hugh, *Cuba or The Pursuit of Freedom* (1971), Updated Edition, Chapter XCII, The Church, 1129, Chapter CV, Cuba Socialista: II, 1350.

- Castro's expulsion of Catholic priests: Thomas, Hugh, *Cuba or The Pursuit of Freedom* (1971), Updated Edition, Chapter CVI, Battle of Cochinos Bay, 1371.

Part Two: Communist Cuba

Chapter Twelve – Living in the Shadows

- Castro declares he is communists: Thomas, Hugh, *Cuba or The Pursuit of Freedom* (1971), Updated Edition, Chapter CVII, Between the Crises, 1373.

- Illiteracy campaign and indoctrination: Thomas, Hugh, *Cuba or The Pursuit of Freedom* (1971), Updated Edition, Chapter CV, Cuba Socialista: II, 1339-1340.

- Soviet technicians in Cuba: Thomas, Hugh, *Cuba or The Pursuit of Freedom* (1971), Updated Edition, Chapter CVII, Between the Crises, 1382.

- Agriculture mismanagement under the Agrarian Reform Institute (INRA): Thomas, Hugh, *Cuba or The Pursuit of Freedom* (1971), Updated Edition, Chapter CVII, Between the Crises, 1374.

Chapter Seventeen – The Cuban Missile Crisis

- Kennedy demands withdrawal of missiles from Cuba: Thomas, Hugh, *Cuba or The Pursuit of Freedom* (1971), Updated Edition, Chapter CIX, The Missile Crisis: II, 1400-1401, Chapter CX, The Missile Crisis: III, 1406.

- Conditions for the withdrawal of missiles: Thomas, Hugh, *Cuba or The Pursuit of Freedom* (1971), Updated Edition, Chapter CX, The Missile Crisis: III, 1413-1414.

- Suspension of US flights: Thomas, Hugh, *Cuba or The Pursuit of Freedom* (1971), Updated Edition, Chapter CXV, New Friends and Old, 1482.

- Number of Cuban children in the US without parents: García, María Cristina, *Havana USA*, 1996, Chapter 1, Exiles, Not Immigrants, 25.

Chapter Eighteen – *Haciendo la Cola*

- Rationing starts: Thomas, Hugh, *Cuba or The Pursuit of Freedom* (1971), Updated Edition, Chapter CVII, Between the Crises, 1377.

- Cuba exchanges Bay of Pigs Prisoner for medical supplies and food: García, María Cristina, *Havana USA*, 1996, Chapter 1, Exiles, Not Immigrants, 33.

Chapter Nineteen – Christmas in Cienfuegos

- The Abolition of Santa Claus: Thomas, Hugh, *Cuba or The Pursuit of Freedom* (1971), Updated Edition, Chapter CI, A Sword is Drawn, 1257.

Chapter Twenty-One – School, *Gusarapos*, and Fellow *Gusanos*

- Cubans from the Mariel boatlift: García, María Cristina, *Havana USA*, 1996, Chapter 2, The Mariel Boatlift of 1980, 62-68.

Chapter Twenty-Three – Rite of Passage

- Exiled Cuban's war against Castro: García, María Cristina, *Havana USA*, 1996, Chapter 4, The Evolution of Cuban Exile Politics, 122-137.

Chapter Twenty-Four – Our Turn

- Restrictions on the Freedom Flights: García, María Cristina, *Havana USA*, 1996, Chapter 1, Exiles, Not Immigrants, 37-39, 43.
  Thomas, Hugh, *Cuba or The Pursuit of Freedom* (1971), Updated Edition, Chapter CXV, New Friends and Old, 1482.

Part Three: In the United States

Chapter Twenty-Five – Finally in Miami

- Cuban refugees arriving in Miami: García, María Cristina, *Havana USA*, 1996, Chapter 1, Exiles, Not Immigrants, 39-40, 44.

Bibliography

1. Didion, Joan, *Miami*, New York: Pocket Books, 1987.

2. García, María Cristina, *Havana USA*, Los Angeles: University of California Press, 1996.

3. Suchlicki, Jaime, *Breve Historia de Cuba*, Los Angeles: Pureplay Press, 2006.

4. Thomas, Hugh, *Cuba or the Pursuit of Freedom*, New York: Da Capo Press, 1971 (Updated Edition).

5. Wyden, Peter, *Bay of Pigs: The Untold Story*, New York: Simon and Schuster, 1979.

Made in the USA
Middletown, DE
20 July 2020